THE ESSENTIALS OF PUBLIC SPEAKING

MASTER POWERFUL STRATEGIES TO COMMAND THE STAGE, SPEAK CONFIDENTLY, AND DELIVER THE SPEECH EVERYONE REMEMBERS, EVEN WITH FEAR & ANXIETY

PROFESSIONAL SKZ PUBLISHING

CONTENTS

 FREE BONUSES

Take advantage of this unique opportunity to guide and motivate you further on your public speaking journey. We're excited to present a specially curated collection of materials, each designed to enhance and amplify your oratory prowess. Embark on this enhanced learning experience to truly elevate your public speaking skills.

Click the link or scan the QR code now to claim your bonuses!

ProfessionalSkillsPublishing.com

 Bonus #1: **Powerful Speeches to Model**

Dissect the artistry of 12 of the most iconic speeches delivered by the world's top influential speakers. These masterpieces, available on YouTube, are a goldmine of techniques and styles to emulate and learn from.

Bonus #2: **Understand Your Audience**

Our 3 uniquely tailored ChatGPT prompts will help enhance audience engagement and save time on your research, ultimately elevating your speech.

Bonus #3: **Capture their Attention!**

Check out our curated list of 48 speech topics, each with 3 sub-topics, designed to spark your creativity, springboard you forward, and ensure your passion and the audience's interest align.

Bonus #4: **Speech Roadmaps**

You will also receive 13 detailed outlines to structure your presentations flawlessly – whether a keynote, wedding toast, or asking for a raise- ensuring your audience remains captivated from start to finish.

Bonus #5: **BONUS CHAPTERS!**

Plus, as a special bonus, delve deeper into the art of persuasion and engagement with 2 exclusive bonus chapters, adding layers of depth and insight to your public speaking repertoire.

- Storytelling: Your Secret Weapon
- The Digital Stage: A New Era

Don't miss out on this opportunity.

Click the link or scan the QR code now to claim your bonuses and continue your journey to becoming an unforgettable speaker!

ProfessionalSkillsPublishing.com

INTRODUCTION

Imagine stepping onto a stage and feeling a surge of exhilaration instead of a wave of anxiety. Standing in front of the crowd, imagine feeling right at home with your shoulders free of tension, confident, and relaxed. Picture yourself delivering your speech with such conviction that the audience hangs onto every word. Throughout your speech, you exude an unwavering sense of self-confidence and boldness, captivating your audience with your passionate and authentic voice that speaks directly to their hearts. As you end your speech, the audience showers you with resounding applause. Who wouldn't? You were simply amazing!

This is the vision of public speaking you deserve, even if it is not the one you have right now. Would you believe 75% of people fear public speaking (Souers, 2022)? Indeed, it is a universal dread that has haunted many of us at some point or other in our lives. That rush of anxiety, the racing heartbeat, the dry mouth– they are all too familiar. However, did you know this fear can hold you back in more ways than you might imagine? For one, the fear of public speaking can hinder your chances of a promotion by a staggering 15% (Zauderer, 2023). Make no mistake—it's a roadblock between you and the opportunities you deserve.

However, here's the catch: 90% of speech anxiety arises from insufficient preparation (Zauderer, 2023). The fear of public speaking, often known as glossophobia, is far more conquerable than you might have ever thought. The nerves that come with standing before an audience are a challenge shared by many, and it's now time to address them head-on.

Do not let the fear of public speaking sabotage your next career move, your wedding toast, or your pitch for that groundbreaking startup. Look, I know it's easier said than done. The butterflies in your stomach seem almost uncontrollable, and the prospect of standing in front of an expectant crowd feels like an insurmountable feat. Nevertheless, here is a secret—a secret that has been shaping the art of persuasion, communication, and audience engagement for centuries: Aristotle.

In the following pages, you will discover the wisdom of the famous Greek philosopher who has profoundly impacted the world of public speaking and communication. Aristotle's five rhetorical secrets are the keys to unlocking your potential as a captivating speaker. They include the following:

- **Understanding your audience:** Tailor your message to resonate with your listeners.
- **Ethos, pathos, logos:** Master the balance between credibility, emotion, and logic.
- **Structure and organization:** Craft your speech for maximum impact and coherence.
- **Language and style:** Choose your words and delivery method with precision.
- **Delivery and presence:** Command the stage with confidence and charisma.

SHARING IN YOUR STRUGGLES

Experiencing the paralysis of public speaking needs no explanation. Choking when confronted with a tough question from a potential investor or your boss is par for the course when fear takes hold. And who hasn't felt their knees weaken as they stand before a room, about to deliver a heartfelt wedding toast?

I get it—really. I understand the catalyst that led you to pick up this book. It's not just about the title—it's about the desire to tackle social anxiety, conquer the fear of public speaking, and finally overcome stage fright. You are at a critical juncture in life where endless possibilities await. And guess what? Seizing that promotion, persuading investors to back your startup, or leaving an indelible mark with your next toast are *all* within your grasp once you master the steps.

In the coming chapters, you will find shortcuts to success that will transform your speaking prowess.

This book is grounded in the profound influence of Aristotle's rhetorical framework on modern-day speaking. As such, you will soon see how these age-old techniques remain as relevant today as they were centuries ago.

Imagine walking into any room and effortlessly capturing everyone's attention. Envision swaying colleagues, students, investors, bosses, and even your family and friends with your words. Picture a life where you are armed with the tools to prepare any speech, captivate any audience, and leave a lasting impression that resonates.

I won't pretend that conquering your fear of public speaking is an overnight journey. However, armed with Aristotle's five secrets and a wealth of practical exercises, trust me—you will make steady, meaningful progress. The destination is a place of confidence and mastery—a place where you can speak your mind without hesitation and stand tall in any situation.

So, are you ready to take that leap? To transform from a hesitant speaker to a masterful orator? Well, swallow that lump in your throat one final time, and let's embark on the path to dynamic and confident public speaking. Your journey starts with the first step to mastery—right here, on the following pages.

THE ART AND POWER OF PUBLIC SPEAKING

As you delve into the world of public speaking, its significance becomes strikingly apparent. The art of addressing an audience is not confined to grand stages alone; it extends its influence into the fabric of our lives—whether it's within the confines of the workplace, the intimacy of our homes, or the camaraderie of friendships. On that note, our first chapter is dedicated to unraveling the enigma that is public speaking—why it wields such immense power and how it can shape our destinies, both positively and negatively. The journey ahead aims to dismantle the chains of fear that often bind us, preventing us from harnessing the potential this skill offers.

THE PHILOSOPHY OF PUBLIC SPEAKING

I want you to imagine the earliest days of public speaking, where one figure stood out with unparalleled power and charisma, leaving an indelible mark on history. Well, this figure was none other than the legendary Greek philosopher Aristotle. Moreover, his ideas continue to resonate throughout Western philosophy, science, rhetoric, and human ethics, shaping how we communicate and influence others.

Aristotle, a visionary thinker, believed in three fundamental factors that set the stage for becoming an influential thought leader. First and foremost, he emphasized that a successful speech should revolve entirely around the audience—not the speaker. This concept speaks to the importance of under-standing your audience's needs, desires, and concerns to engage them effectively.

The second key factor Aristotle championed was addressing topics that bring "happiness" to the audience. Indeed, by tailoring your content to resonate with your listeners' interests and emotions, you create a powerful connection that keeps them engaged and receptive.

Thirdly, Aristotle advocated for speaking in the *language* of the audience. This means selectively using language, for one, but also using idioms and references that your listeners will easily understand and relate to. In doing so, you bridge the gap between yourself and your audience, fostering a deeper level of connection.

However, Aristotle's brilliance did not stop there. He introduced the powerful persuasion framework known as ethos, logos, and pathos. This framework forms the cornerstone of effective communication, allowing speakers to craft compelling arguments that resonate with their audience on multiple levels.

Rhetoric, the art of persuasion, is driven by Aristotle's insights. This framework continues to shape our daily communication in various contexts. Whether you are delivering a business presentation, a motivational speech, or even engaging in a casual conversation, the principles of rhetoric play a role in how you convey your ideas and influence others.

Now, let us uncover the five "secrets" of Aristotle's persuasion framework, known collectively as the five canons of rhetoric (Mind Tools, n.d.):

1. **Invention:** This refers to the process of gathering and developing ideas for your speech. It involves careful consideration of your audience's needs and interests, as well as selecting the most persuasive arguments.
2. **Arrangement:** Organizing your speech logically and engagingly is crucial. As such, Aristotle advised structuring your speech with a clear introduction, the main points, and a compelling conclusion.
3. **Style:** How you present your message matters. Using language that resonates with your audience, employing vivid imagery, and maintaining an appropriate tone all contribute to the effectiveness of your speech.
4. **Memory:** While this may seem antiquated in our digital age, memory was essential for ancient speakers.

Memorizing key points allowed them to engage the audience more effectively, enhancing the impact of their message.

5. **Delivery:** How you deliver your speech greatly influences its impact. Your tone, gestures, eye contact, and overall presence contribute to how your audience receives your message.

Aristotle's insights into public speaking and persuasion remain timeless, offering a treasure trove of wisdom for modern speakers. So, whether you are raising a toast at a celebration or delivering a pivotal speech that demands action, remember Aristotle's principles and the enduring power of effective communication.

SPEAKERS WHO CHANGED THE WORLD

Public speaking continues to be a vital skill in modern times, bridging the gap between the past and the present. Indeed, it has remained a potent tool for conveying ideas, motivating action, and shaping public opinion in many arenas of modern public life. The art of persuasive communication has been wielded by numerous famous speakers to influence and captivate audiences. Let us explore some examples of renowned figures who have utilized this skill effectively (Whitworth, 2023):

- **Ronald Reagan:** The 40th President of the United States, Ronald Reagan, was known for his eloquent speeches that resonated with numerous Americans. His communication style combined warmth, optimism, and a clear vision for the future. Reagan had the ability to make complex ideas accessible to a broad and diverse audience, fostering a sense of unity and shared purpose.

- **Barack Obama:** As the first African American President of the United States, Barack Obama was an engaging public speaker. In his "Yes We Can" victory speech, his use of anaphora in the phrase "Yes we can" created a chant-like momentum that transformed the speech into a collective call to action, embodying hope and change.
- **Martin Luther King Jr.:** A pivotal figure in the American Civil Rights Movement, Dr. Martin Luther King Jr. employed the power of words to inspire change and advocate for equality. His iconic "I Have a Dream" speech remains a prime example of how a well-crafted speech can ignite social transformation, leaving an undeniable mark on history.
- **JK Rowling:** In her 2008 Harvard Commencement Speech, the highly acclaimed author of the *Harry Potter* series captivated her audience with a masterful combination of humor, personal vulnerability, and insightful reflections. Rowling's ability to connect with her audience and convey her message in a relatable and engaging manner has made her one of the most influential and beloved writers of our time.

Today, public speaking goes beyond physical stages to encompass virtual platforms and digital media. Social media, podcasts, webinars, and online video platforms allow individuals to share their thoughts and ideas with a global audience.

Also, in today's world, public speaking involves not only delivering speeches to large audiences but also engaging with diverse communities on various topics. Whether delivering TED Talks, participating in panel discussions, or creating informative content online, influential public speakers can still sway opinions, raise awareness, and drive action.

Public speaking today requires adapting to new mediums. Furthermore, it also requires understanding the dynamics of virtual communication and tailoring messages for specific audiences. However, the ability to capture attention quickly, convey messages concisely, and evoke emotion remains essential. Moreover, in a world saturated with information, speakers who can deliver authentic, relatable, and impactful presentations are bound to stand out.

With all this being said, it's clear that today's successful public speakers have connected the art of rhetoric from the past with the technological advances of the here and now. While I am sure many of these speakers come to mind, it must be said that influential speakers like Reagan, Obama, Rowling, and King have left a critical legacy as we have entered our modern digital age, inspiring current and future generations to communicate effectively and make a meaningful impact on society.

WHY DEVELOP THE SKILL OF PUBLIC SPEAKING

In an era characterized by rapid technological advancements and ever-changing communication mediums, I cannot stress enough that the art of public speaking remains a cornerstone of success. On that note, let's explore how public speaking can empower individuals and transform lives:

- **Career advancement:** Public speaking skills are a coveted asset in the professional realm. The ability to confidently convey ideas, influence others, and lead discussions can set you apart and propel your career forward.
- **Idea sharing:** Public speaking provides a platform to share your thoughts, innovations, and ideas with a broader audience. As such, it is a catalyst for knowledge dissemination, sparking inspiration and driving positive change.
- **Boosting confidence:** Standing in front of an audience and delivering a compelling message boosts self-assurance and self-esteem. Overcoming the fear of public speaking can also translate into newfound confidence in various life situations.
- **Strengthening critical thinking:** Crafting and delivering speeches requires deep analysis and organization of your thoughts. Public speaking cultivates the art of structuring arguments and conveying complex ideas with clarity.
- **Exercising deductive reasoning:** Public speaking necessitates anticipating audience reactions and

tailoring your message accordingly. This process hones your deductive reasoning skills and enhances your ability to connect with diverse audiences.

- **Expanding networks and enhancing leadership:** Engaging in public speaking exposes you to diverse individuals and opportunities. It cultivates leadership skills as you navigate conversations, inspire change, and influence groups.
- **Informing and persuading:** Effective speakers have the power to inform, educate, and even persuade audiences to adopt new viewpoints. This skill is crucial for driving social, political, and business changes.
- **Encouraging audience change:** Compelling speeches can inspire audiences to reconsider their beliefs and behaviors, fostering positive transformations on both personal and societal levels.
- **Driving personal development:** Public speaking challenges you to continuously refine your communication style, adapt to different audiences, and refine your message. This growth extends beyond the stage and ultimately enriches your personal journey.
- **Improving interpersonal communication:** The skills acquired through public speaking—such as active listening, empathy, and adaptability—greatly enhance your everyday conversations, leading to stronger relationships and better understanding.
- **Building connections:** Speaking engagements offer opportunities to connect with like-minded individuals, mentors, and collaborators. These connections can propel your career, creativity, and personal growth.

THE ESSENTIALS OF PUBLIC SPEAKING | 19

- **Creating lasting memories:** The moments when you deliver a captivating wedding toast, share an unforgettable idea at work, or spark thought-provoking discussions become memories that resonate with you and your audience.

In a world overflowing with information, public speaking remains a potent tool to captivate hearts, stimulate minds, and ignite change. As such, I encourage you to embrace the challenge with enthusiasm, as mastering this art can open doors to many opportunities, enrich your personal growth, and leave a deep impression on the hearts and minds of those fortunate enough to hear your words. So, step onto that stage with fervor, express your ideas with passion, and watch as the world transforms before your very eyes!

OVERCOMING GLOSSOPHOBIA

Glossophobia (glä-sō-ˈfō-bē-ə)– the fear of public speaking- is that elusive hurdle we must conquer to truly shine on stage or in front of an audience. So, let's break it down to get acquainted with it—and learn how to overcome it.

Glossophobia is more than just a tongue-twister to pronounce. It is a social phobia, one of the three primary types that can throw a wrench into our aspirations of becoming confident speakers. Typical glossophobia symptoms can range from sweaty palms and a racing heart to a shaky voice and that persistent feeling of "stage fright" that can put a damper on your presentation (Syed, n.d.).

What is behind this fear? Why does glossophobia rear its ugly head when we are faced with public speaking? Well, to put it bluntly, the causes can be diverse. Perhaps it's the fear of judgment or the worry that we will stumble over our words and look foolish in front of others. It could also stem from past negative experiences that have left a lingering scar on our confidence. The anticipation of potential embarrassment can be a powerful force, indeed.

And guess what? This fear is so deep-seated that it reveals itself in the very core of who we are when we are diagnosed. You can imagine it as a mirror reflecting your deepest fears and insecurities. But there is a way out of this daunting labyrinth!

Therapy is a lifeline for those who find themselves gripped by debilitating glossophobia. It is an option that should be seriously considered, and it complements the journey you are embarking on by picking up this book. However, exposure therapy is where the magic truly happens! You cannot conquer a fear if you are avoiding it like the plague. That is where the forthcoming chapters come into play.

So, get ready to embrace progress and push those fears aside because, from here on out, it is all about embracing stressful situations. That's right—we are going to chip away at that anxiety and break free from its hold. And what is this secret? Preparation and practice. These are your ultimate tools to conquer the stage and captivate your audience.

Why go through all this trouble? Because public speaking isn't just about addressing a crowd—it is a gateway to thought leadership, professional growth, successful pitches, building your personal brand, and even delivering a heartwarming wedding toast. However, there is a caveat! You cannot tap into these exciting avenues until you have shattered the chains of social anxiety that are holding you back.

And here is an eye-opener: You cannot just "crush" glossophobia like any old phobia. Why? Because it is not a specific phobia—it is a social one. So, to conquer it, you must tackle the underlying beast of social anxiety head-on. Only then can you truly liberate your ability to speak confidently and engage your audience.

While the journey to overcoming your fears might seem like a steep mountain to climb, remember that the view from the top is worth every step. Embrace exposure, master preparation, and engage in a bit of practice, and you will transform into a charismatic speaker ready to conquer any stage in no time!

INTERACTIVE ELEMENT: EXPLORING YOUR FEARS WORKSHEET

Instructions

Take a moment to reflect on your fears and anxieties. Then, use this worksheet to identify and record what triggers your fears, how they make you feel, and where you feel discomfort in your body. This exercise can help you gain insight into your fears and take the first step toward disarming them.

- **Fear trigger:** Write down a specific situation, event, or thought that triggers your fear or anxiety. It could be related to something you are pursuing or a challenge you are facing.
- **How it makes me feel:** Describe the emotions and feelings that arise when you think about or encounter this fear trigger. Be honest and specific about your emotional response.
- **Physical discomfort:** Indicate where in your body you feel discomfort or tension when faced with this fear trigger. It could be a tightness in your chest, a knot in your stomach, a racing heart, etc.
- **Possible root cause:** Consider whether there is a deeper reason or past experience that might be contributing to this fear. Reflect on whether any past events or beliefs have shaped your current reaction.
- **Relevance to your goals:** Think about how this fear is connected to what you are seeking or pursuing, as mentioned in the book. Does this fear have any influence on your progress or actions?
- **Positive reframe:** Challenge the fear by thinking of a positive or empowering perspective related to the fear trigger. How might you view this situation differently in a way that reduces anxiety?
- **Action steps:** List one or more actionable steps you can take to confront or manage this fear. These could be small steps that gradually help you build confidence and overcome the fear.

Conclusion

By completing this worksheet, you have taken an essential step toward understanding and disarming your fears. Remember that recognizing and addressing your fears shows strength and growth. As such, you should use the insights you have gained to advance your journey of self-discovery and personal development.

Each thought, fear, and experience you have had has left an impression on your mind. However, the thing is, you will not have much success using Aristotle's framework or the inspiration from Martin Luther King Jr.'s powerful speeches if you cannot crush your fear first. So, let us focus on turning social anxiety into something you can work on in the later steps.

2

SPEAK UP: CONQUERING GLOSSOPHOBIA

S tanding in front of an audience confidently and assuredly does not come naturally to many people. In fact, if you find yourself crushed under the weight of social anxiety and, as a result, are unable to speak publicly due to its harrowing clutches—let me assure you that you are *certainly* not alone. Nearly 90% of those who suffer from social anxiety also find the words becoming trapped in their throat when in front of an audience, as well as the bubble of panic rising in their stomach when tasked with a mere speech (31 Fear of Public Speaking Statistics (Prevalence), n.d.).

I won't lie; overcoming the fear of public speaking isn't easy. As we move into Chapter 2, you won't exactly be mastering the inherent genius of Aristotle just yet, but what you *will* do is learn some foundational secrets to crush your fear. Sound good?

SOCIAL ANXIETY

The nagging fear restraining you from delivering that perfect toast or speech and even simply sharing your ideas in a small working group is a fear shared among millions. What can be done to help you start overcoming this immense fear?

You might wonder whether you can erase your social phobia entirely, scrubbing its existence from the plane of your life. The unfortunate news is that no eraser will succinctly remove social phobia from your life. However, you can take steps to reduce that fear, transforming it from a massive beast to a minuscule bother.

"How can I do that?" I hear you asking.

Well, the first consideration that should linger in the forefront of your mind is that social phobia is not quite a *specific* fear. What do I mean by that? Simply put, I mean that social phobia is a broad form of anxiety rather than a fear of something specific itself. You don't necessarily fear the crowd or speaking; it's the concept of "speaking publicly" that causes the anxiety. With me so far?

To make this more straightforward, let's think of someone who *does* have a specific fear, such as arachnophobia. This is another pervasive fear within our society, and it typically involves a specific fear—*spiders*. So, someone with this phobia might be afraid of spider bites or the feeling of a spider crawling across their skin, for example. When it comes to public speaking, however, no specific fear is present—the simple concept of "public speaking" itself is an anxiety-inducing scenario.

With that in mind, how does this help us conquer the fear? In a sense, being able to view glossophobia and social phobia through this particular lens is helpful because it contributes some rational thinking to the mix. Anxiety is innately an irrational experience, but by recognizing it as such, the table is turned. Once you recognize this viewpoint of the fear of public speaking, you can begin to crush that fear once and for all.

Alright—now that we have that out of the way, I would like to take a moment to break down overcoming social phobia into steps that can make a difference. After all, it is only through organizing yourself, following a framework, and practicing your framework and outlines relentlessly that you can genuinely kiss this fear goodbye once and for all. Now, take a look at this more cohesive three-step process:

1. **Know what it is that you are speaking about.** Before you set out to embark upon public speaking, know what it is you are talking about. The more you care about a topic, the less likely you'll overthink or stumble.
2. **Formulate a framework for your speech.** You do not have to plan out your speech word for word meticulously; in fact, some of the best speeches rely heavily upon improvisation. However, it is essential to have a rough outline for your speech, one that follows a comfortable and cohesive order.
3. **Practice, practice, practice.** Once you know your topic and have a rough idea of what to say, practice that speech relentlessly. Practice in front of an imaginary audience and pour your heart and soul out as if you

were giving the actual speech. Then, by the time the speech rolls around, you won't stumble.

Now, that might sound too good to be true, like you are staring at something so simple that it cannot possibly work. If this is how you feel right now, I encourage you to give these methods a chance and observe the results organically. Those three steps will, in time, become your most beloved companions in the realm of public speaking.

In the midst of your public speaking adventure, I know that the temptation to focus on the audience will overtake you. You cannot help but think about their eyes staring back at you, the perceptions racing through their heads, and worse, what happens if your speech is purely meaningless to the crowd? Overcoming this aspect of social phobia is as simple as training your mind to think of the speech and not the audience—at least at first.

Why exactly does this work? Well, think about the last time you witnessed an excellent speech. Think about how your brain latched onto the new information being thrown at you, leaving you mentally on the edge of your seat in anticipation. I will bet that you did not notice the words that the speaker stumbled on, nor did you notice them wipe their sweaty, shaking palms on the sides of their pants as they spoke. This is because the mind is trained to focus on new information.

While you are presenting to an audience, their minds will do the same thing. The new information becomes the focal point of the speech, not your nerves or anxious actions or even the presentation of said new information in some cases. So, while a gripping and compelling speech will captivate audiences more than a reel of information would, your nerves go largely unnoticed. This means that you genuinely don't have to worry about whether or not an audience can tell how anxious you are—they usually cannot.

Fear is the byproduct of a biochemical reaction. In cartoons and other TV shows, audiences always seem to be throwing rotten tomatoes at a speaker who dares to waste their time with something subpar. Obviously, this is not how it happens in real life; no tomatoes are being hurled, and hardly any judgment is being passed. So, where does this fear truly come from?

Fear, as it turns out, is a natural response within our brains that originates from a survival mechanism. We avoid ventures that scare us to prevent harm, and yet hardly anyone has been harmed due to simply giving a speech. Wading through your social phobia, you might ponder what the cause of this fear is and why you have it in the first place. The answer is simple: there likely *is not* a reason. Sometimes, social phobias are the result of fight-or-flight responses that make us feel anxious. As such, there is not always a clear-cut reason behind your phobia.

At the same time, you might have specific worries or doubts bounding around inside your head. Did you know you can challenge and conquer specific thoughts, fears, and scenarios that might scare you from making the perfect speech? Seriously —it is possible!

CHALLENGING NEGATIVE THOUGHTS AND WORRIES

For some people, social phobia takes the form of a racing heart, a thin sheen of sweat coating the forehead, and bubbling anxiety that has no correlating thoughts or worries. The anxiety simply... *exists*. But for others, their glossophobia manifests as a current of specific thoughts and worries—detailed considerations of "what if" or what could go wrong. This section offers tips for those struggling with excessive worries and thoughts to keep them at bay.

Now, there is a term for the type of thinking that leads to your worries. They are called "cognitive distortions." A cognitive distortion is an irrational thought or belief that centers around how you perceive the world or yourself. If you have ever thought that, for example, you were a failure because you did not meet a goal, then that is an example of an unproductive cognitive distortion that holds you back.

Cognitive distortions, believe it or not, tie directly into a fear of public speaking. Interlacing your thoughts are these distorted beliefs, doubts, and perceptions that negatively influence your ability to speak publicly. And beyond merely stopping you from making a wedding speech or pitching a new idea at work, cognitive distortions can be immensely detrimental when it comes to your mental and physical well-being. For example, those who suffer from cognitive distortions are more likely to experience isolation and low self-esteem, hindering socialization and provoking mental illness (Rice, 2021).

In the previous chapter, you got an intimate look at some of the thoughts and fears that hold you back. Now, it is time to become aware of such thoughts and fears. By understanding the cognitive distortions and generalized fears that provoke you to avoid sharing, speaking, and more, you will be able to overcome these distortions' effects.

Together, let's take a look at some of the most common distortions that ground people in negativity and ultimately stop them from reaching their goals:

- **Mental filter.** Imagine winning a million dollars, but there is a caveat—you have to wait a year to cash it in. In this instance, a mental filter would involve having such a narrow view of one isolated part of the situation that it becomes negative to you. So, rather than being elated over the million dollars, you come to have negative thoughts due to the year it will take to receive the money.
- **Magnification and minimization.** Consider how a magnifying glass makes small things much, much bigger; the eye of a needle can become a canyon. Well, this is how magnification works. If you magnify your thoughts, something that is not such a big deal can transform into a massive problem right before your eyes. Minimization, then, is the polar opposite—when you consider something that is a big deal (usually an accomplishment) to be irrelevant.
- **Discounting the positive.** Undoubtedly, positive occurrences exist within your life. However, for

someone who regularly discounts the positives, these positives can become immensely difficult to see. Discounting the positives involves minimizing positive aspects in your life to focus on the negative instead. This can, of course, be incredibly harmful to your ability to be satisfied with life.

- **Emotional reasoning.** Emotional reasoning describes the fallacy many people fall into, wherein you assume that your feelings are equal to reality. For example, you may feel like your speech will crash and burn, and therefore, you assume that that is the reality of the situation. In reality, though? It's not!

- **Imperative statements.** Imperative statements include words like "should" and "must." This remains a common cognitive distortion because it serves to be a critical way that many people hold themselves back. They believe that if something does not go as it "should," then it is a complete failure. The reality is that there are degrees of success not accounted for by such imperative statements.

- **Personalization.** Sometimes, events and obstacles that have little or nothing to do with us personally can make us feel bad. Something falling over across the room can quickly spiral into a reflection of your failings if you are not in the right headspace. This is a typical example of personalization—a fallacy that involves attributing something unrelated to yourself or your worth.

What do all of these cognitive distortions have in common? Well, the answer is that all of these distortions have the villainous ability to tear you down, wrecking your chances of success as a speaker.

What this means is that overcoming the hurdles of cognitive distortions is your best chance at not only overcoming your social phobia but also becoming an assured speaker. Cognitive distortions are just that—distortions. They serve no positive purpose in our lives, and you can overcome them in part by challenging them as they appear. When you notice the creeping hands of distortion strangling your goals and aspirations, take a step back and think: *How can I prove this distortion false—and what purpose does it truly serve me?*

Concerning the thoughts hindering our progress toward over-coming glossophobia, the completing factor is *rumination*. Have you ever thought something over and over so often that it made you feel insane? And each time you thought about it, did the situation slowly worsen? That, in a nutshell, is rumination. Rumination is one of the most common ways that a simple worry can spiral into a whirlwind of anxiety.

In modern times, rumination has become so common that most people think nothing of it; however, if you genuinely aspire to trump your glossophobia once and for all, you must primarily become aware of *when* you are ruminating. Indeed, just noticing the rumination process in and of itself can be transformative. You can go from an anxious mess to a confident rockstar overnight if only you learn to spot rumination.

From there, you can effectively *stop* rumination by asking yourself a few questions, such as these:

- Is this thought helpful to me?
- Is this thought getting me closer to my goals?
- Does thinking it over help me to prepare, or is it just making me more nervous?
- Are these thoughts grounded in reality, or do they stem from a "what if" line of thinking?
- Does the thought I am having fall into a cognitive distortion?

Upon asking yourself some of these questions about your thinking, you might find that what you are doing is ruminating.

When you challenge the thought processes that hold you back —including cognitive distortions and rumination—you come one step closer to truly fighting an articulate battle, one where your glossophobia stands no chance in blocking you from your goals.

THE INTROVERSION BUBBLE

The road to overcoming the main obstacle of social anxiety does not end there. Something else that must be considered is something known as the "introvert bubble." For the vast majority of individuals who find the creeping clutches of glos-sophobia holding them back, it is also true that they consider themselves introverts. And while introversion itself is not bad, how we respond to introversion can make for a negative sting on one's life.

The notion of being an introvert is often misinterpreted. What most people likely don't know is that just because you are not fond of a roaring crowd does not mean you are an introvert—at least, not necessarily. Introversion has nothing to do with how much you love a crowd. In fact, a crowded party with dozens of guests can be your idea of a dream, yet you may be introverted simultaneously.

In all truth, an introvert derives energy or inspiration from solitude—not necessarily someone who *prefers* it. For many people who consider themselves introverted, this attribution is based on the fact that standing in front of a crowd and sharing ideas candidly can be a horrifying, nail-biting experience. Yet, if everyone who was weary of sharing their ideas publicly were indeed an introvert, then only a slim percentage of the population would be extroverted!

If you consider yourself an introvert, that also has no bearing on how "good" you are at public speaking; after all, an extrovert cannot assert that they are bad at being alone—that is not how it works. Introversion merely reflects what it means to recharge and, thus, is not where your skills lie.

So, what does this have to do with your overbearing fear? Well, as it turns out, someone who is trapped within the confines of the introversion bubble is unable to sustain personal growth. Yes, you heard me correctly. The introversion bubble hinders you from growing personally and overcoming obstacles.

If you consider yourself an introvert, you have probably waved a white flag regarding specific activities. Conceding that you will never be a partygoer or someone who flourishes in an intensely social setting, you have likely solidified the idea within yourself that various concepts are out of your reach. As such, this stunts your personal growth dramatically.

When you embody this personality trait, you tell yourself that you *cannot do something*—all because of a self-imposed label. In this way, the introversion bubble is like a sticky fly trap that withholds you from your dreams. The fact is that life is full of difficulties—for everyone! You cannot reasonably expect life to be simple at every turn. When you trap yourself inside the introversion bubble, the notion of challenge—the essence of what compels us to grow—is warded off in its entirety.

Fortunately, avoiding the introversion bubble is simpler than expected. All it involves is finding the strength to get out of your head and ditch those ruminating thoughts. For some, though, this may be easier said than done. I recommend revisiting the questions in the last section to defeat rumination and push yourself to do new things. Even if something seems "scary" or out of character for you, it's alright to do it—pushing yourself out of that introversion bubble is the only way to truly attain growth.

Another method for bursting out of that bubble is becoming more flexible. The walls of a bubble might seem malleable, giving pressure if you push on them, but that is just a mirage; those walls are inflexible, and they *will* crumble. The only real way to outlast this illusion is to become more flexible. Doing so involves allowing yourself to try new things, even if it feels like setting yourself up for failure. This also entails trying things that aren't "you," as this will allow you to grow outside the confines of the strict rules that the introversion bubble has imposed.

Furthermore, it might be time to shed the label altogether if you struggle to break free from the introversion bubble. I hear you gasping and clutching at your chest at the mere thought of this, but consider it for a second: Has labeling yourself as an introvert ever truly positively changed your life? If not, then it may be serving as an unnecessary constraint that prevents you from achieving what you aspire to do in life—specifically, preventing you from breaking down the barriers of glossophobia and the accompanying social anxiety.

Now, after hearing all of the information I shared with you throughout this chapter, you might be curious— what can be done to help you face your fears and challenge the thoughts that block you from greatness? Well, we are going to consider this next.

OVERCOMING SOCIAL ANXIETY

Look—facing your fears while challenging the thoughts that hold you back is, without a shadow of a doubt, one of the hardest things you can do. At the same time, though, it's also one of the bravest. When you find the inner strength to over-come these roadblocks, a world of opportunity opens up, including the world of public speaking. In order to overcome the social anxiety that provokes your glossophobia, you are going to need a few tactics.

"Flooding" is a dynamic tactic I espouse for those grappling with glossophobia. It operates on the fundamental psychological principle that fears are learned behaviors and, with the right strategy, can be unlearned. Consider the roots of your fear: is it the result of an innate discomfort or an unpleasant past event? Regardless of the origin, your fear has been ingrained through social conditioning. Flooding counters this by saturating your routine with public speaking tasks, challenging the validity of your fear by proving, time and again, that the dread is disproportionate to the reality of the situation. Yes, flooding is an upfront confrontation with your phobia. It might stir the pot of your deepest anxieties, but it also fast-tracks the realization that the fear, while emotionally tangible, is practically unfounded. The world, as you will find out, remains steadfast as you speak.

You will notice a shift in your perception of public speaking by consistently placing yourself in the spotlight. The more you speak, the more the fear fades into the background, replaced by growing self-assurance and skill. Flooding not only diminishes the fear response but also sharpens your oratory capabilities through varied interactions and audience feedback. It's an open secret that the path to becoming a polished speaker is paved with the bricks of resilience and learning. Flooding, although intimidating at first glance, is a transformative journey that equips you with coping mechanisms for anxiety, such as strategic breathing and mental prep. While it's true that not every speech will echo with applause, each word you utter is a step away from fear and a step closer to becoming a confident, compelling public speaker. With professional guidance, flooding becomes not a trial by fire but a calculated ascent to eloquence and poise.

Furthermore, overcoming glossophobia can also be managed with these four tools:

1. **Preparing for difficult questions.** A major source behind the fear of speaking publicly for many is the question, "What if someone asks me a question and I do not know the answer?" Naturally, the solution for this is to prepare in advance for difficult questions. Research questions that may be asked in similar speeches and understand what a response would look like. Your preparation does not end there; rehearse your answers as if they were a part of your speech.

2. **Garner some perspective.** It may feel awkward initially, but try recording yourself as you rehearse your speech. In this way, you can play your recording back and understand whether any nervous habits appear, how to improve your speech and any common pitfalls you are subject to. Overall, this will ensure that you are much more prepared.

3. **Visualize yourself succeeding.** Many people don't know this, but your brain often cannot distinguish between imagination and reality. Therefore, you can essentially "trick" your brain into calming down and envisioning success by genuinely putting yourself in a

mental scenario wherein you have already accomplished your speech flawlessly.

4. **Accept your anxiety.** A small amount of anxiety is normal. When you try so hard to force "negative" feelings out of your life, it makes you even more anxious in the long run. As such, it is crucial to accept your anxiety rather than treat it like a force to cast out altogether.

By working with these skills, you can master your social anxiety fully and completely.

INTERACTIVE ELEMENT: IDENTIFYING RUMINATION

Instructions

As you endeavor to speak confidently, understanding how to identify your ruminating thoughts is vital. For this activity, you will grasp the identification of your ruminating thoughts in order to overcome them. Use this worksheet to guide you:

- **Feelings**: When it comes to public speaking, what do you feel emotionally and physically? Write these factors down.
- **Thoughts**: Are there any particular thoughts accompanying the feelings you just listed? Write those down as well.

- **Cognitive distortions**: Finally, try to analyze those thoughts that you just described. Decide whether they are based in reality or have evidence to support them and if those are helpful thoughts. See if you can name a specific cognitive distortion associated with your thoughts.

Conclusion

Friedrich Nietzsche said "[i]nvisible threads are the strongest ties." As you walk through Aristotle's five principle framework, your invisible threads hold your psyche together. It starts with reinventing yourself, overcoming self-doubt, and exuding confidence to challenge and reduce those fears from the first chapter and the ruminating thoughts from this one.

3

INVENTION: THE BUILDING BLOCKS OF CONFIDENT COMMUNICATION

I t is not uncommon to fear public speaking, and you are not alone in this. However, seeking help to overcome this fear is not very common. In fact, only a small percentage of individuals, only 8%, seek help to develop beyond this fear (31 Fear of Public Speaking Statistics (Prevalence), n.d.).

Feeling hopeless and helpless is a fate that troubles many people throughout their lives. When it comes down to it, it is something only you have the power to change.

Interestingly, studies find that one's comfort and confidence in speaking in front of others increases as one ages (31 Fear of Public Speaking Statistics (Prevalence), n.d.). Even still, that is a large portion of people who *never* become comfortable confronting their fears or standing in front of a crowd.

The point is that you do not have to fall victim to the same fate. Even if you don't necessarily seek professional help, know that the very act of reading this book is still an act of seeking and obtaining help in some form.

The beginning of genuinely overcoming your fear involves reinventing yourself through the development of confidence, practicing exercises that help you go into public feeling secure, and crushing the self-doubt that makes you victim to your fears. So, without further delay, let's get you inspired and confident enough to press forward!

INVENTION

In order to understand Aristotle's first secret to public speaking, we have to take a closer look. What is invention? What did Aristotle mean by using this seemingly simple term?

Well, the powerful secret of invention involves questioning whether something you say is factual. Invention in the context of public speaking involves using reliable resources to research your argument. In contrast, many people wrongly believe that invention involves pulling ideas out of thin air and fabricating the very contents of one's speech from start to finish. But make no mistake, this is not what invention is about.

At its core, invention invites quality; when you engage with invention, it is necessary to think about the *quality* of your belief in what you are saying. For example, what values influence your speech and its content? What informs it? Does what you say align with your personal views, the views of your company, or something else?

There are other factors to consider when it comes to Aristotle's first canon of rhetoric. First, start by asking questions to yourself such as:

- **What is the subject?** Considering the subject matter in detail is, believe it or not, an aspect of invention that's often overlooked. In order to make a great speech *and* feel confident about it, it is necessary to know what the topic of said speech is.
- **Can you define the topic and the elements that compose it?** This question involves understanding whether you genuinely know what you are talking about. If someone in the audience asks for clarification, you must know your subject and what it involves.
- **Have you selected an outlet for your message?** In other words, how will you convey the message to an audience? A speech is not always face-to-face; in modern technology, Zoom presentations or Instagram livestreams pose valuable options for conveying a message.

Additionally, invention necessitates that you know your audience. Suppose you step out onto a stage in front of an audience of first-time mothers. In that case, understanding their hesitations, anxieties, and concerns about parenthood will allow you to advertise this up-and-coming car seat company more aptly, for example. The point here is that when you know your audience, you can adequately speak to them in a way that leaves a lasting impression on their memory.

Understanding the basics of invention is a start, but how can you walk through its rhetorical steps? To do so, you must master self-confidence, release self-doubt, and be authentic in your connection to the audience, all of which we will delve into next.

RELEASING SELF-DOUBT

Mastering the art of invention begins with a journey of releasing self-doubt. As you set foot upon this seemingly treacherous path to releasing everything that makes you feel attuned to the words "I cannot," strive to bring those thoughts from the last two chapters—the fears and what made you *feel* those fears. This is vital, as releasing self-doubt begins on the back of self-awareness.

How you speak to yourself is referred to as "self-talk." For someone held back by the harness of self-doubt, it is crucial to analyze how you talk to yourself—out loud, in your head, or otherwise. Your doubts about your abilities stem from a place of negative self-talk, and defeating that habit is where self-awareness ties in.

So, what is it you need to do, exactly? To fend off these negative thoughts that drown you in doubt, you have to recognize that you are having negative thoughts in the first place. After all, you must be aware of the fire before you can put it out. There are a few steps to recognizing the sheer existence of your patterns of negative self-talk:

1. When you notice a negative or doubting thought enter your mind, stop. Just take note that a negative thought has occurred without trying to judge it.
2. Think about what you were doing, saying, or feeling before the negative self-talk occurred. This is going to be what *triggered* the negative self-talk.
3. Repeat this process whenever you catch yourself thinking one of these thoughts.

The more you engage with these three simple steps, the more you will come to recognize patterns in what triggers a negative thought; you will understand, for example, whether a particular person, activity, or even song makes you feel doubtful about yourself.

After that, you have to charge forward and dispute the thought. At the moment, a negative thought can feel like the end of the world; your simple "I will never make a good speech" assertion can transform into a rigid rule that you have placed upon yourself right before your eyes. This is what we are going to change. Why? Because negative thoughts do not deserve such power over you.

When you feel the overbearing blanket of negativity, it can be hard to see through to the light of a situation—but you will have to force yourself to do it anyway. So, for starters, see if you can find any evidence to the contrary, as this will help disprove the negative thoughts bounding through your head.

For example, let us say the thought that "I will never make a good speech" is your negative thought. Has there ever been a time when someone commended you on a speech or even congratulated you? Or the opposite: Have you ever made a demonstrably bad and truly horrendous speech? Chances are, you haven't. Rationalizing your negative self-talk in this manner is the key to disputing such thoughts.

Furthermore, you can add two tools to your toolkit to overcome negative self-talk: the dynamic duo of "ability-talk" and "effort-talk." Ability-talk takes the lens that you are *already* good at something, even if you truly are not. Remember: the human mind cannot easily distinguish belief from reality, which means that telling yourself, "I am so good at public speaking," can convince your brain that this statement is entirely factual.

Effort-talk is similar. It involves speaking in a manner that conveys your willingness to put effort into a task. For example, telling yourself that "I will try my best" for a speech empowers you to put in the effort to do your best. Subliminally, this also assures you that you are good enough and do not have to stretch to meet the standards anyone else places upon you.

Releasing self-doubt also involves substituting any absolutes in your speech. Absolutes are phrases that indicate that something is always a shade of black or white when the reality is that several shades of gray come into play. The following are examples of absolute statements you might find yourself repeating:

- I will *never* make a good speech.
- I *always* mess up my public speaking.
- They are *always* judging me when I am speaking.

When you allow these absolutes to fester within your head, you lose the ability to release the self-doubt they facilitate. So, to put it simply, this means you have to move away from absolutes in your thinking. Take a look at these revised versions of the statements above:

- One day, I will make an *amazing* speech.
- I made a *few* mistakes, but I tried my best!
- My audience is *actually* cheering for me to succeed.

See how those absolutes became shades of gray that no longer confine you to a rule? By abandoning the rigidity of absolute statements, one can shed the coat of self-doubt and truly grow.

It is crucial to understand that self-doubt can be countered with an antidote. This remedy has the power to diminish even the most monstrous form of self-doubt, leaving it powerless. Self-love is the secret that nurtures the defeat of self-doubt.

It might sound like a joke, but honestly, we are conditioned by society to suppress the powers of self-love. However, self-love is the polar opposite of self-doubt, and so by inviting self-love into your life, you create an impenetrable shield between yourself and those negative thoughts. Finding the courage to fight doubt with compassion is one of the strongest, most positive changes you can make if you truly desire to free yourself from self-doubt.

REINVENT YOURSELF WITH GRATITUDE

As we inch closer to the line of invention, crushing self-doubt, and inspiring confidence, there is one unstoppable superhero we need to meet along the way: gratitude. Gratitude is so important because, without it, you cannot see your good qualities, nor can you truly crush self-doubt or inspire reinvention that dissolves your self-doubting tendencies.

One of the best parts of embracing an attitude of gratitude is that it allows you to mine for diamonds of positivity that can overshadow any spots of negativity in your life. You see, gratitude has the striking ability to boost our emotional well-being and happiness. With such a positive mindset, it can be hard to even think about the impact of negative self-talk or self-doubt.

You can also use gratitude as a means to silence self-doubt in action. When you have a thought that's less than appreciative of yourself or where you are in life, counteract it with gratitude for how far you have come and what you have accomplished. This kind of reframing can prevent self-doubt from negatively impacting your life.

Now, in order to make gratitude a regular practice in your life, try keeping a gratitude journal. A gratitude journal is one of the quickest ways to see a pile of wonder appear before your eyes. While most gratitude journals focus on being grateful for what you have or the world around you, let us give this one a little spin: Focus this gratitude journal on why you are grateful for *yourself*.

Journaling about your skills, abilities, and accomplishments allows you to appreciate your worth as a human being. You can even use prompts, such as the following, to inspire you as you journal:

- What are three things about myself that I appreciate the most? Why do these qualities or attributes make me proud?
- Reflect on a recent accomplishment or achievement, no matter how small. How did my efforts contribute to this success, and how can I celebrate it?
- Describe a challenging situation I have overcome. How did my resilience and determination play a role in my victory?
- List three aspects of my physical health that I am grateful for. How can I continue to care for and appreciate my body?
- Think about a mistake or setback from my past. How have I grown or learned from this experience, and how can I be grateful for the lessons it taught me?
- Who are the people in my life who support and love me unconditionally? How can I express gratitude for their presence and contributions to my well-being?
- What three things do I enjoy that bring me joy, peace, or a sense of accomplishment? How can I make time for these activities more regularly?
- Reflect on the personal growth and self-improvement I've experienced over the past year. How can I express gratitude for my journey of self-development?

- Write a letter to my future self, expressing gratitude for the person I am today and the progress I hope to make. What words of encouragement and appreciation can I offer my future self?
- What positive affirmations or self-love mantras resonate with me? Write them down and explain why they have significance in my life.

If you challenge yourself to journal for even 3 minutes a day about how grateful you are for yourself and your accomplishments, you will start to notice the demon of self-doubt shrinking further and further from your consciousness.

Okay, now let us return to the core idea of invention. How does reinventing yourself with gratitude for confidence tie in with invention?

First, the way that you speak to yourself matters. As I mentioned earlier, the self-talk you engage in plays a significant role in how you feel about yourself and your abilities. If you only ever fill your mind with negative self-talk, you will naturally not feel confident in your abilities; however, if neutral or positive self-talk becomes your new norm, you will be a powerhouse of confidence.

The fact of the matter is that if you have been invited to speak publicly or have the opportunity to do so, you probably have something of value that can be added to the pitch, conversation, or situation. Otherwise, someone else would have been asked or invited to speak.

In this instance, the best course of action is to try and place the information ahead of yourself. For this moment, consider the information you have to convey more important than your nerves, doubts, and anxiety—because, in many cases, this helps you avoid being held back by these things.

Being nervous, scared, or worried does not devalue the message you are trying to share. A stammering individual speaking compelling and useful words is much more worthy of an audience's attention than a confident person saying nothing of substance, after all. Keep this in mind: The people you are speaking to *want* to listen; if not, they would not be there. Remember that as you stand in front of the crowd, *they are all rooting for you.*

Mantra Rituals to Pump You Up

All of this talk is good, but you need something *great* to help you confidently walk on stage. That is where mantra rituals come into play. A mantra ritual uses repetition and self-talk to soothe you. If repetition, soothing language, and comforting words calm you, this is perfect.

Find a word or phrase, such as "I am calm and present," that connects to a positive, small goal for your speech. Then, look in the mirror and chant that mantra to yourself. It might feel silly at first, but you will find yourself more assured and comfortable once you get into the habit of it.

AUTHENTICITY AND VULNERABILITY

Authenticity and vulnerability are like twins; together, they can also help you with the invention stage of unleashing your brilliance. Consider some of the best speeches and presentations that you have ever witnessed. I am willing to bet that the instances of that speech that spoke to you the most were those driven by authentic interaction and the willingness to be vulnerable. These are the skills we will help you hone to ramp up your performances.

If you have ever tried to imbue authenticity into a speech, you might have found yourself standing in front of a mirror, rehearsing a joke, blunder, or mistake that humanized you to the audience. While humanization is desirable, the mistake that you are making with this rehearsal is, well, rehearsing it at all! In other words, genuine authenticity does not come from practice.

Be yourself on stage. If you make a mistake in your speech, trip over your words, or crack a joke that does not land, the audience will find you endearing—someone authentic and vulnerable that they can trust, someone just like them. This leads to how you have to allow yourself to become vulnerable on stage.

Vulnerability does not come easy to everyone; it involves bearing your soul to a crowd of strangers, showing them a part of yourself that you might not even be familiar with fully. It can be frightening—something you fear adding to the already horrifying task of public speaking. Nevertheless, vulnerability can be the key to invention, helping your audience connect with you completely and honestly.

Now, you might be wondering how you can unlock authenticity and vulnerability on stage; after all, it is not like that is something you can narrow down to a four-step process, right?

It is! To unleash your authenticity and vulnerability for genuine crowd connection, follow these four steps:

1. **Play to your strengths.** The first step is playing to your strengths because using them makes it much easier to speak from an authentic place. For example, if you are a wonderful storyteller, include a gripping personal anecdote in your speech. Incorporate those strengths, and they will naturally form connections with the audience, promoting a more engaging speech.
2. **Find some balance.** Going into a speech full of rehearsed enthusiasm is just as likely to turn off a crowd from paying attention as complete disinterest can; you have to find a balance between your emotions and enthusiasm to captivate the crowd perfectly. Connect your verbal and nonverbal communication to what you are saying, and allow those facets to drive natural balance in your communication.
3. **Be purposeful.** Speak like you mean it, and ensure your personality shines through. At the same time, be careful to avoid over-manufacturing yourself for the crowd. They want someone honest and genuine to connect to, and that is only going to happen if you do not just sell your topic but yourself, too.

4. **Have passion.** Your passion for the topic is infectious; if the crowd sees your genuine passion and enthusiasm for what you are talking about, they will feel the same passion.

Your authenticity and vulnerability have to shine through in a speech for the audience to understand that they should be poised on the edge of their seat, ready for a thrilling presentation. With those four steps, you are well on your way to being the speaker they crave.

PRACTICING IN THE MIRROR

You do not want to go out to your speech's big day without rehearsing and re-rehearsing your speech. Whether practicing in front of a mirror or your family or even giving the speech to your beloved pet, you have to know what to practice for that time to be fruitful. So, what do you need to focus on for the perfect rehearsal?

It begins with taking measures to manage your nerves. Your nerves are no doubt one of the most debilitating aspects of the speech. By dusting off some methods for quelling your tense nerves, you can get off on the right foot:

- Learn about controlled breathing and how to do it, as this will help you feel more at peace as you stand behind the curtain, ready to present your speech. For example, you can practice square breathing, inhaling for four seconds, holding for four, then exhaling for

four, holding for four, and repeating, a cycle that
soothes the mind and steadies the nerves.

- Pick out some music to listen to on your way to the
location of your speech. The right music can put you in
a positive headspace, whether driving, taking a bus, or
even boarding a plane.

- Select a mindfulness exercise or two you can engage
with on your way there or as you prepare to walk out
on stage. For example, you can practice a sensory
engagement exercise where you identify five things you
see, four you can touch, three you can hear, two you can
smell, and one that you can taste to draw you to the
present moment.

- Try not to consume too much caffeine—if any—before
your speech. Caffeine is a stimulant, which can cause
you to feel nervous—more nervous than you already
feel. On top of that, caffeine is a diuretic, which can
leave you with an overactive bladder to go with your
nerves.

Also, remember that your audience does not know that you are
nervous; unless sweat is pouring from your forehead and you
are shakier than a bobblehead on the dashboard of a car, your
nervousness will not be the first thing on the audience's mind.
Before your speech and as you practice in the mirror or in front
of someone else, try getting into the swing of soothing your
nerves using the methods I just provided you.

Remembering to rehearse your posture is the next dynamic of
an excellent speech. Posture, of course, refers to how you stand

and even walk around up there on stage, and it matters greatly when it comes to what the audience takes away from your speech. Think about it: Someone hunched over a podium exudes far less confidence and trust than someone standing tall yet relaxed.

The fact is that bad posture acts like a barrier between you and the audience. On the other hand, when you have a clear and robust posture, your audience can be more receptive to what you are saying. Keep your arms uncrossed and relaxed by your side, your back straight, and your head up high as you speak to the audience; these, especially in combination, are the key to a confident and assertive posture. An open posture signals to your audience that you're comfortable, confident, and open to engagement.

For many people, standing upright with their arms uncrossed by their side, especially in front of a group, makes them feel very vulnerable. And it's true, in a certain sense—you are being *open*. Because it can feel uncomfortable, though, this way of standing is something worth practicing and getting comfortable with. As you can imagine, it does not come naturally to many people.

Also, do not let something physically come between you and your audience. A podium, a laptop, or even a microphone stand can create dissonance between you and the audience. Instead of letting these items block you, step to the side and allow yourself and your audience to be face-to-face, with nothing between you but air and opportunity.

From there, it is time to focus on eye contact. Now, many people wrongly assume that because the audience is several feet away, they cannot see your eyes—this is typically untrue. Never doubt the power of your gaze. Therefore, you should allow yourself to make eye contact with the crowd and select members to lock eyes with. Do not stare them down, however!

And that is not all—think about infusing your speech with a touch of humor. If there is a prop you have dropped or if you trip over a microphone cord, make a joke about it and move on. By refusing to fixate upon mistakes and instead turning to humor, you can keep the audience's focus without drawing attention to minor mistakes. This is a perfect blend of vulnerability and authenticity for your speech.

INTERACTIVE ELEMENT: REFRAMING WORKSHEET

Instructions

Negative thoughts, as discussed throughout this chapter, can contribute to self-doubt and a lack of confidence in your speech. In order to overcome this, try filling out the following worksheet to reframe your thoughts. You can even give this a shot weekly:

- Is there significant evidence that proves my thought to be correct?
- Is there evidence that disputes my thought?
- Does my interpretation of this situation lack evidence?

- If I talked to my friends about this situation, what would they think?
- How is the situation different from a positive lens?
- Is this matter going to be important a year from now? Five years from now?

Conclusion

Roy T. Bennet said "[i]f you can remove your self-doubt and believe in yourself, you can achieve what you never thought possible." And this is very true. So, on that note, start practicing your authentic self, confident mirror talks, and empowering reinvention. Then, you can move to the arrangement canon in Aristotle's framework to further your confidence and public speaking skills.

4

ARRANGEMENT: CRAFTING THE ARCHITECTURE OF YOUR SPEECH

Preparation matters more than you might think when making a compelling speech that genuinely connects to an audience. Sure, it is possible to deliver a wildly successful impromptu speech. However, this possibility is likely pretty slim and, thus, something you should not rely on because success is not the typical outcome of an unprepared speech.

Indeed, a lack of preparation is responsible for the fact that 90% of people struggle to perform on stage, becoming anxious or failing at their speech altogether (31 Fear of Public Speaking Statistics (Prevalence), n.d.). This fact underscores the importance of preparation.

Another interesting consideration to note is that audience engagement skyrockets when you invite members to speak or interact with the speech in some way; at the same time, this is not something you can achieve without careful preparation.

This is one of the many reasons why careful planning is necessary to attain complete and succinct audience engagement.

Proper planning is crucial for delivering a good speech, and it all starts with preparing yourself for the presentation and effectively conveying your ideas. Even Aristotle emphasized the importance of planning in public speaking and acknowledged that every speech requires careful preparation.

I understand that preparing a speech can be nerve-wracking. That is why we have eight steps to help you get ready. While this will not be the outline you will use to form the final speech, it does break down key moments and steps you must prepare before you devise an outline.

UNLEASHING ARRANGEMENT

Aristotle's second canon of rhetoric is arrangement, which focuses on delivering influential and memorable speeches. The arrangement of your speech determines how you sell your idea, influence others, and prepare for debates that may arise. However, what makes a good preparation for speeches, whether at a wedding or to pitch an idea to a room full of investors (or even the boss who may promote you)?

Let's step through them now:

Step #1: Plan Your Speech Around the Occasion

It is essential to understand that certain occasions require an appropriate type of speech. For instance, you cannot attend a wedding and use a toast as an opportunity to pitch a business proposal. Similarly, you cannot use a wedding toast to request a promotion at work. Although this may seem obvious, understanding the occasion is one of the first considerations you need to arrange your speech. As Aristotle would advise, understanding an event's tone and point will guide you toward the speech you need to present.

So, in order to help you narrow down your occasion and what that means for your speech, there are a few questions that you can ask:

- Is this a formal event or one that's more casual?
- Will those in attendance be people whom I know or strangers?
- What is the purpose of the speech that I am making in the context of this event?

These questions are excellent for narrowing down the formality and connection that can be anticipated from a given occasion. In tailoring your speech to the occasion rather than hoping they match, you come to the table prepared and ready with something appropriate.

Step #2: Pick a Topic or Purpose

Now, no good speech is complete without a topic or a purpose. A topic may arise naturally when you think about the occasion you are presenting for. If not, ask yourself what the speech is about. Where are you and why are you there: at a conference, a school assembly, or your best friend's wedding? *That* would be your topic.

Once you have a topic narrowed down, you can begin to learn more about it. The best presenter is at least slightly more knowledgeable about the topic at hand than the audience. Beyond that, interest is of the essence—if you do not seem interested in the topic, your audience will not be either. Plain and simple.

Furthermore, think about *why* you are presenting your speech. "My boss made me" or "my cousin asked me to" are not answers that highlight the purpose. Are you trying to inform someone, persuade them, or even entertain them? Understanding the *why* helps plan a speech that is appropriate and interesting for your audience.

Step #3: Compiling Content

Of course, you cannot speak if you have nothing to say! Therefore, the next step of mastering arrangement involves gathering content that will be used in your speech. Sometimes, such as if your boss asks you to present data, you will already have that content ready. In other cases, the brunt of the research and consideration falls to you. This means you must dive headfirst into the world of research, untangling what you will say and its relevance.

An excellent tip for your compilation stage of arrangement involves gathering more information than you need. A speech should only contain the best of the best information; if you are presenting the benefits of a new product, irrelevant or uninteresting information will only distract your audience from the key message. If you gather together more information than you need, you can sift through what you have to pick only the best out of the collection.

Step #4: Organize the Contents of Your Speech

Chances are, you did not compile your information in the exact order that you will present it—actually, you probably *should not* present it in the order in which you compiled it. Careful planning also means that you have to intricately arrange the contents of the speech now that you know what the speech will contain.

For most speeches, there is a standard format you can follow. First, tell your audience what you are going to be talking about. Then, get into the heart of the speech, and lastly, finish off with a summary. This allows your audience to know what to expect, consume the content of your speech more readily, and then hear a snappy summary of it all again to keep it fresh in their minds.

Step #5: The Introduction

Your speech needs a compelling introduction that reels the audience in and keeps them captivated. Of course, you do not have to start with the most exotic or original line to keep your audience's ears and minds open; instead, all you need is to know your audience.

First off, in order to know your audience, consider their age. Does your audience come from a diverse age range, or are you presenting to a group from one particular age range? It will also serve you well to consider the culture, financial background, and family situations that your audience may fall into.

The point is that once you know your audience, you can hit them with a provocative question, a shocking statistic, a powerful quote, an amazing anecdote, or another introduction that truly knocks their socks off, keeping them enticed throughout your time on stage.

Remember, the introduction of your speech is your first chance to make an impression on your audience. A captivating opening can draw your audience in, setting the stage for a powerful and engaging speech. Whether you choose to open with a quote, a question, or a statistic, ensure that it aligns with your key message and resonates with your audience. After all, the best introductions are not just heard; they are felt. They don't just inform; they inspire. They set the stage for a speech that is not just listened to but remembered.

Weaving a captivating introduction is akin to carving the face of your sculpture. It's the first thing your audience sees. It reflects your speech's soul. It commands attention, incites curiosity, and builds anticipation. With a well-crafted introduction, you will not only capture your audience's attention but also their hearts and minds, paving the way for a speech that truly resonates.

Step #6: Visual Aids

Now, not every excellent speech needs a visual aid; you can certainly make a memorable one with nothing but yourself and some preparation. However, in situations where visual aids make sense, integrating them can help your audience envision your end goal. In other words, a few well-placed visual aids can compel your audience to understand your vision with total precision.

Think about a textbook you might see in a classroom. For a biology textbook mapping out a bodily structure, the textbook might bring up a chart or diagram next to the text that's relevant to the diagram. This reinforces the learning in the reader's mind while simultaneously clarifying the diagram and the text with one another. Then, during an exam, one can recall the material by drawing their mind back to the corresponding imagery. A visual aid in a speech serves a similar purpose.

Based on this, you should only present the visual aids in your speech as you talk about the relevant subject matter. For instance, a chart expressing a visual representation of a statistic should only be visible when mentioning the statistic; otherwise, the audience becomes mentally numb to that visual aid—and potentially any other visual aids throughout your speech.

A common mistake when presenting a visual aid is speaking "to" the visual aid. Many presenters make the mistake of facing the screen of their PowerPoint presentation rather than their audience, which creates a sense of dissonance. Now, it is okay to occasionally glance at the visual aid, even pointing if needed, but most of your focus should *always* be on the audience. This means you must have your visual aid memorized! And be able to speak to it and its details without reading from it.

Also, consider having hard copies of your material to distribute to your audience, especially if it's appropriate for your setting. Don't assume everyone can see your presentation on a screen. It can be helpful to visit the location beforehand to understand where the screens and stage are in relation to the audience. Additionally, providing physical copies of your material can help jog your audience's memory at the end of your talk.

Step #7: Phrasing

Alright, so the next step involves working with the phrasing of the speech. Now that we have the message, purpose, introduction, and various cues and aids ready, it is important to think about *what* you will say and *how* you will say it on the big day. This will make delivering or ending the speech much more natural and fluid.

One mistake that people commonly make is attempting to memorize the exact phrasing of a speech in order to recite it perfectly on the day of delivery. Trust me on this one—the audience can tell if you are providing a play-by-play of a pre-written speech. We intrinsically engage with particular intonations and vocal habits upon recital that make the speech seem mechanical and distant—and that is not what you want.

Instead of doing this, you will want to use something called "extemporaneous delivery." This means you walk into the speech well-prepared and versed in what you will say, but you do not have the exact phrasing memorized and ready to go. Instead, the wording is spontaneously created live and in the moment. This is the best way to deliver a natural-sounding and compelling speech from the bones of preparation.

Step #8: Rehearsal

The final step to mastering speech arrangement is rehearsal. This is where you rehearse your ode to the audience in the mirror, your family, or even your pet over dinner. Rehearsal is also the stage where you hammer out struggle points and prepare for mishaps, which we will focus on more in Chapter 5.

Altogether, these eight steps are the key to a successful arrangement. Indeed, this is the framework you need for any speech, whether a proposal to clients at work or a commencement address. With this compelling framework, you are sure to succeed. Even with these steps outlined, though, you may still have some questions—ones crucial to helping you improve upon applying these steps. Let us go ahead and address those now.

KNOWING YOUR AUDIENCE

By definition, the introduction to your speech is the first thing your audience hears. The first few seconds are a make-or-break part of your speech that can reel your crowd in or disinterest them entirely. In order to truly empower yourself through Aristotle's arrangement tactic, you have to make an introduction that paves the road to a truly great speech. The secret to doing so? You remember: *knowing your audience.*

The good news is that a few simple tricks can amplify your speech and awareness of your audience, minimizing the amount of research necessary to reach the same end goal. Let's consider what you need to know to make this your reality as you captivate the crowd.

The Three Keys

In order to know your audience *and* communicate with them in a meaningful way, you need to do three things:

1. Make sure your speech's topic, particularly your introduction, appeals to them.
2. Understand the approximate amount of knowledge your audience already has about the topic.
3. Use inclusive topics that can appeal to broad demographics, including being aware of when to include cultural considerations.

It really is that simple! In order to help you truly understand each of these three keys, I will expand on them further.

It all begins with ensuring the audience is interested in your speech. Sometimes, you can present a speech to someone who does not care about your topic and still make a bang if you go at it from the right angle; however, you will be far more successful if you present a topic your audience cares about.

And that's not all—you should also try to understand *why* they care about that topic. For example, let us say that you are pitching a new shoe company that prides itself on minimalism and nonslip bottoms. Now, are you pitching to nurses or fast food workers? There is a stark difference between the two, and by understanding the motivation, you can tug on their heart-strings a little more.

Of course, avoiding assuming the audience is just like you is also a good idea. The same reason that you care about a topic might not align with why they care about that topic, and that's fine—but you have to know *why* they feel differently and *how* they feel differently.

After that, you must aim to understand how much the audience already knows about the topic. And this is a fragile balance. If you talk to them as if they know nothing, but they are, in fact, professionals, then your approach may seem condescending. Conversely, if you talk to your audience like they are experts when they are inexperienced about the topic, they likely will not follow you too well, and from there, they will lose interest in what you are pitching.

This is one area where you might have to do some research or even ask someone who would be an ideal audience candidate what they already know. Doing so can give you a good lens regarding balancing technical terminology alongside examples and anecdotes.

Finally, consider the cultural differences your audience may have that make you an outsider. This does not just apply from country to country; someone in a different city can have an entirely different culture than you do. Leveraging that culture to understand norms and language can make your speech far more interesting to an audience.

Preparing for a Specific Audience

So, let us say you have a specific audience in mind—one that you know some basic details about and need to prepare for as you craft your speech. Now what?

First, do at least some research in advance if you can; try to contact the person organizing the event and see if they know anything about the audience or their expectations. This will provide you with a launchpad to begin your research. Furthermore, if you know you are presenting to a specific company or person, look them up beforehand.

If you cannot research the audience, it might be a good idea to greet them at the door if possible. In doing so, you can mingle and learn more about them—empowering you to use that information within your speech to make adjustments on the fly.

It might also benefit you to be familiar with the layout of the room in which you will be presenting. It might not seem important now, but see if you can look at the stage, meeting room, or other area ahead of time. By familiarizing yourself with the space, you can make sure of how best to lay out visual aids and engage with the audience, depending on the size of the space.

By including these methods in your speech arrangement process, you are on the right track for a compelling speech your audience can connect to.

CHOOSING A TOPIC

From the moment you begin arranging your speech, you will probably be wondering how exactly you are going to choose a topic around which to center it. At this stage, authenticity is the glimmering key that serves to unlock the doors to an amazing speech.

If you have complete freedom over the speech, authenticity will come from connecting the speech to something you feel confident about.

So, how can you truly ensure that the speech has some alignment with you while also speaking to your audience in a captivating manner? Believe it or not, it all starts with your core values. Before you select a topic, take some time to write down your core values—even if they do not seem relevant to the speech at all. Some tips to help you isolate your core values include the following:

- **Consider the people you admire.** Whether it be Abraham Lincoln or your mother, consider who you admire and why you feel that way about them.
- **Reflect upon your most meaningful experiences.** Evaluate which life experiences have left an indelible mark upon your memory and why you think that is.

- **Write down as many ideas, philosophies, or concepts as you find essential.** From there, you can consolidate them into groups or a central sentence expressing your values.

Once you have identified your core values and highlighted which ones are nonnegotiable, there are three questions you should ask yourself before solidifying your topic.

1. **How much do I know about this topic?** In order to make an impactful speech, your audience has to consider you to be credible. Coming in with an armload of knowledge is the best way to assert credibility, and it helps if you have at least some preexisting knowledge on the subject.
2. **Is this a topic I am passionate about?** Someone passionate about a topic will deliver a more exciting speech nine times out of ten than someone who does not care about the topic. Passion influences all manner of your delivery, after all.
3. **Is this something that's going to interest the audience?** Remember that your speech is not for you —it is for the audience. If it is about a topic they have little interest in, they will likely tune you out early on.

Once you have everything in order, you can begin selecting and consolidating a purpose and topic for the speech. When we think about the purpose of a speech, the answer to the big "what's the point" question, you can give three short answers:

to persuade, entertain, and inform. Every speech will fall into one of those three answers.

Your purpose, and isolating it early on, is instrumental to your speech and its quality. The purpose of a speech is not only to help you remain more organized but also to give you a central goal that you can aim to accomplish by the speech's conclusion. As a result, the audience can walk away and feel that they have either accomplished something or learned something valuable.

ORGANIZING YOUR TOPIC

After selecting your topic, it is time to lay out the main points of your speech. The perfect number of main points for a speech is not set in stone, although keeping the number low is a good idea. It can be tempting to lay out 15 main points for an audience, but then they may become overwhelmed, and the information will not stick. As such, an excellent format to follow is three main points, with evidence and a rebuttal for each— allowing you to address possible opposition before it happens.

At the same time, your main points must not appear disjointed; you have to find unity among them. Finding unity among the main points of your speech provides an unforgettable level of cohesion that the audience can continuously be drawn back to for the greatest impact.

A delicate relationship between separation and balance needs to be maintained simultaneously. While keeping your main points distinct, you should also balance each one and talk about them evenly. Some speakers get so caught up in their favorite point that they neglect the others, which can let the audience down.

Using parallel structure within your points for your speech is also wise. Parallel structure, or parallelism, is a powerful tool in speechwriting that enhances clarity and rhythm and can make your message more memorable. It involves using the same pattern of words to show that two or more ideas have the same level of importance. This can be achieved by starting each clause or sentence with the same part of speech, maintaining the same tense, or ensuring that nouns, verbs, and modifiers are used consistently.

For example, consider a speech on the benefits of environmental sustainability. To employ parallel structure effectively, you might structure your points like this:

"Environmental sustainability:

1. Preserves our natural resources for future generations,
2. Promotes biodiversity and the abundance of wildlife, and
3. Encourages self-sufficiency and reduces reliance on non-renewable energy."

Each point begins with a verb in the present tense, creating a pleasing rhythm that reinforces the message's cohesion. When points in a speech mirror each other in this way, the repetition makes the content more engaging and more accessible for the audience to follow and recall.

In contrast, without parallel structure, the points may feel disjointed:

"Environmental sustainability is important because it:

1. Preserves our resources for future generations,
2. Keeping biodiversity in abundance is another reason, and
3. It also increases our self-sustainability."

The lack of consistency in the format can make the speech more complicated to follow and weaken the impact of your words. By aligning your sentence structure, you guide your audience through your points with a clear, strong drumbeat that drives home your message. Use parallel structure to give your speech a rhythm that resonates with your audience, making your message heard, felt, and remembered.

PERFECTING VISUAL AIDS

Earlier, I mentioned how helpful visual aids can entice an audience to focus on your speech. Now, I want to investigate this further and drive home some great ideas in this department.

Again, not every speech *needs* a visual aid, but a visual aid can be more than helpful for both you and the audience in following the *story* of your speech. Visual storytelling is a worthy skill for anyone looking to flourish at public speaking. However, what *is* visual storytelling exactly? As the name would suggest, visual storytelling involves using visual aids, cues, and gestures to transport the audience into a world of your own—one where you run the show.

You might think that visual aids only come in the form of boring flow charts and dull PowerPoint presentations, but that isn't the case at all. When you master the art of visual story-telling, you become aware that it is an entire world of opportunity just waiting for you to explore it. Indeed, visual storytelling is versatile and comes in many forms that can take your speech to the next level.

Visual storytelling transcends the boundaries of traditional narrative by incorporating visual elements that engage and captivate the audience. When delivering a speech, you must adapt these principles to the stage. This adaptation involves using gestures, props, or visual aids to create a sensory experience that complements the spoken word. By doing so, you craft a compelling narrative that paints a story vividly in the listener's imagination, fostering a memorable and impactful connection.

In addition, you should never forget the data—especially in presentations or pitches. Your audience will not want to hear every statistic about what you sell or offer. However, some compelling diagrams that make everything clear and visually based can leave a mark on your audience members. Nothing says "successful presentation" like an audience in awe from some mere data points.

Visual aids can also be perfected by focusing on showing rather than telling. Think about it: If a presenter tells you you are five times less likely to crash using their new car technology than a competitor's, that's good! But if they *show* you the evidence through charts or diagrams, including videos of the safety features, they have taken their speech from good to *great*. As such, adding a visual component to your speech—one that is logical and relevant—can make a difference in the quality of your presentation.

As you work on your arrangement, remember that visuals are far more than just what lingers on a screen. We live in a visual world and a world that is abundant in technology, meaning you have no excuse *not* to take advantage of it.

Many things can play a role in visual storytelling, from what you put on the screen to the handouts you give to the audience to how you dress. Never be afraid to use your resources —and do not hesitate to be creative! Your audience will appreciate it!

INTERACTIVE ELEMENT: DESIGNING VISUAL AIDS

Instructions

This activity focuses on helping you build a visual aid for an event like a wedding speech or toast. Feel free to follow along or reframe the activity to fit your needs for any given speech. The instructions are as follows:

1. Gather essential information about the wedding, couple, and venue before crafting your visual aid. This includes details about the couple's love story, the

      wedding theme, and any significant elements you want to highlight.

2. Select a pivotal moment or scene from the couple's love story to highlight in your visual aid. It could be their first meeting, a memorable date, or the proposal. Ensure this moment holds emotional significance.

3. Write a narrative that describes the chosen moment in vivid detail. Use descriptive language to create a mental image in the listener's mind. Include sensory details such as what the scene looked, smelled, and felt like. This narrative will be the heart of your visual aid.

4. Now, design the visual elements that will accompany your narrative. These could be photographs, illustrations, or a simple graphic representing the scene. Ensure these elements enhance the story and help your audience visualize the moment.

5. Choose fonts and colors that complement the wedding theme and the emotion you want to convey. Elegant script fonts and soft, pastel colors often work well for wedding-related visual aids.

6. Consider the layout of your visual aid. Arrange the narrative and visual elements in an aesthetically pleasing manner. You might want to use a digital design tool or create a physical collage, depending on your preference and skills.

7. Incorporate personalized messages and quotes that relate to the couple and the moment you are framing. These can be words of encouragement, well-wishes, or famous love quotes that resonate with the scene.

8. Review your visual aid and narrative for clarity, grammar, and emotional impact. Make sure everything flows well and evokes the desired emotions.

9. Practice your wedding toast with the visual aid to ensure it fits seamlessly into your speech. Adjust your delivery as needed to synchronize with the visuals.

10. During the wedding toast, display your visual aid with confidence. As you reach the part of your speech related to the framed scene, engage the audience by referring to the visual aid. Speak from the heart and allow the narrative and visuals to enhance the emotional impact of your toast.

And voila! You have a compelling visual aid that can be used in your speech and a format to follow to create a visual aid for any event.

Conclusion

John Ford said, "[y]ou can speak well if your tongue can deliver the message of your heart." With those words in mind, find your values, align your speech's purpose, and inspire yourself to speak more confidently by preparing everything you can with the eight simple steps in this chapter—planning, picking a topic, compiling your content, organizing content, writing the introduction, planning your visual aids, working out phrasing, and then rehearsing. Some of those steps, of course, warrant some in-depth tips. So, with that said, let us see how you can create your Aristotle-style secret with communication and rehearsal.

YOUR OPINION MATTERS

"If I went back to college again, I'd concentrate on two areas: learning to write and to speak before an audience. Nothing in life is more important than the ability to communicate effectively."

— GERALD R. FORD

I hope that by now you are excited about the opportunity to embrace brilliance in public speaking by harnessing Aristotle's five rhetorical secrets. Timeworn yet more pertinent than ever, these techniques are testimony to the changeless nature of effective communication. Reaching your audience and making a big impact is ultimately about viewing public speaking as the life-changing experience that it is.

How many times in your life have you struggled to make your voice heard or to make authentic connections with people? When you are called upon to give a public speech, it is a unique opportunity; a golden window of opportunity to share a message about something you are already passionate and knowledgeable about. And there is an audience out there that is eager to be entertained and informed; one that wants to hear your story and laugh, feel, and discover alongside you.

I mentioned that around 75% of people fear public speaking, thinking that they lack an innate talent or gift. However, as found by Zauderer and other researchers, 90% of speech anxiety lies from simply being unprepared. And I hope that by now you have seen how factors such as authenticity and vulnerability – qualities we all share – can help you make a big impact on your audience.

If this book is helping you speak up, take the steps you need to nip social anxiety in the bud, and craft your speech with vivid detail, then I hope you can share your enthusiasm with other readers.

By leaving a short review on Amazon, you can let others know that great public speakers aren't born, they're self-made.

Your words will encourage others to embrace and practice the skills they need to speak their hearts and minds to an audience that also yearns to make intellectual and emotional connections.

Let someone else know that they don't have to fear standing at a podium and sharing who they are. Authenticity is everything when you wish to be heard and, in turn, listen to what others have to say.

Scan the QR code for a quick review!

5

STYLE: THE SYMPHONY OF SPEECH

P icture yourself at a concert. The music starts, and the room fills with a diverse range of sounds from the orchestra. The booming drums, the soft whisper of the flute, and the rich melody of the violin - all blend to create a harmonious symphony. Now, let's transpose this orchestra to the public speaking stage, where your voice plays all the instruments. It can whisper, boom, and carry a melody - and learning to manipulate your vocal elements is like mastering the art of conducting a symphony.

Aristotle's third element involves mastering your voice and choosing to speak your style!

THE BASICS OF STYLE

Before choosing your style, we need to dig into the basics of style itself. Indeed, let us take a look at some of the background information you need to bear in mind.

Again, style is Aristotle's third canon of rhetoric. But what exactly is it? Simply put, style refers to how well you deliver your speech. It refers to what you say, how you say it, and its quality. For example, take a look at the two examples below, where each speaker uses their unique style:

- Speaker 1 comes onto the stage and greets the audience before launching into a technical analysis of some research. While the research is relevant to the topic, this speech is being given to a group of consumers—not professionals in the field. They walk away confused, even feeling stupid because of the speech's presumptions.
- Speaker 2 comes on stage and speaks to the same audience but emphasizes passion and conviction. This speaker's words seem to have personal importance, and any technical terms are defined. The speech follows a logical flow, only including technical terms or analysis when it naturally comes up.

If you saw those two speakers on stage and were a member of that audience, chances are you would trust Speaker 2. However, there are also instances where speaker one is preferred. This is why style is so important; your style helps the audience connect to you and can make or break their trust in you.

Why Your Style Matters

I honestly cannot overstate how much your style matters, but I am sure you are still wondering why that is the case. Well, beyond merely looking better in front of an audience, style matters for two key reasons:

1. Your style matters because miscommunication and conflict may occur if it contrasts heavily with the audience.
2. Your style matters because it informs the context of your visual aids and other factors discussed in Chapter 4.

If you don't spend time perfecting your style, you cannot make an awe-inspiring speech.

Different Styles to Explore

Before you endeavor to find or craft your style, you should take the time to explore some of the established styles and what they look like. This will allow you to consider which style fits best with your personality and your speech's purpose. Below are a few different styles, some of which you may want to consider emulating:

- **The teacher style.** When you embody a teaching style, you aim to instruct and explain. With outstanding content and the need to cram it into an allotment of time, you must balance your ability to connect with the crowd with your insightful information. Think of a teacher who can't keep their class captivated; this is a common struggle for teachers when it comes to style. In order to make a great teacher, one must focus on information *and* connection.

- **The motivator style.** Someone who embodies the motivator style has the goal of inspiring change. They primarily want those to whom they are speaking to take action. The motivator style, as the name suggests, is inherently motivating! However, those with this style often suffer from losing energy as the speech goes on. This is certainly something to be mindful of.

- **The storyteller style.** One of the most popular styles, storytellers, use emotion to connect with the crowd. This style is so popular because it's the voice of many great speakers throughout history, which is a testament to its effectiveness. Having a clear and focused point is the key to achieving success. Stay on track, and you'll shine like gold.

- **The visionary style.** Finally, we have the visionary style—someone who envisions a better world, along with the role that an audience can play in making that dream a reality. Visionaries compel audiences to see change that does not exist, thus facilitating actual change. The major drawback of this style is that many speakers are unclear on *how* to make that change—and the audience can tell.

These styles can be adapted to meet your needs and the particular point of a speech. You can even blend methods to meet specific goals.

Styles to Avoid

Despite all of those intriguing styles just mentioned, there are still a few that you should try to *avoid* at all costs—each in its unique way. For example, take a look at the following styles that you should avoid falling prey to:

- **The passive style.** If your speech style appears too passive, the audience may not take you seriously due to your lack of assertiveness.
- **The aggressive style.** If you head into the speech aggressively, it is likely to offend your audience.
- **The passive-aggressive style.** Mixing the passive and aggressive styles, this tone does not go over well with audiences—it seems noncommittal and dispassionate.
- **The overly assertive style.** As the name suggests, this style can come off as pushy and can thus discourage the audience.

Choose your style before focusing on anything else. Then, your context, visual aids, body language, and tone will follow from what you know the four styles offer.

BUILDING UP COMMUNICATION

Now that we have covered all the styles you can choose from (and the ones you should avoid at all costs), it is time to look at how you can build your communication skills using your selected style as a springboard.

First things first, and though I have mentioned this before, it is worth mentioning again: Do not memorize your speech word for word. Seriously. I can confidently say that walking into a speech with it fully memorized is one of the worst mistakes you can make. Rather than memorizing everything you want to say, come prepared with cue cards or a bare-bones script of your speech. This allows for a perfect blend of spontaneity and audience engagement.

In addition, don't rush your speech. One of the worst feelings in the world is getting through your speech and feeling confident, only to find that you still have 15 minutes left to fill. Solution? Make sure you take your time through the speech, fully enveloping your audience with your introduction before expanding on your main points. Between this and your practice rounds, you are bound to fill the time well.

Another vital communication skill is understanding when your audience's attention begins to slip away. If your audience begins to tire as you get into the heart of your speech, remember it may not be anything personal. The average attention span is growing shorter and shorter, which is why you need to come prepared with content to zest up the speech as you deliver it.

Communicating and following these tips can pave the way to an excellent ending by remaining confident and sticking to your main points. Sticking to the predetermined outline you have made will help your speech remain cohesive while being spontaneous and relaxed with your pace, which will further emphasize that you are a credible speaker in the eyes of your audience.

Furthermore, it would help if you made it a point to use *inclusive* language. While you might not identify with someone who needs or uses inclusive language every day, you never know who in your audience might appreciate some inclusive language on your part. By using inclusive language, you can further command the audience's respect. Some common ways to avoid unintentional exclusion include the following:

- **Using gender-neutral terms and pronouns where possible.** For example, supposing that only men will do a specific job or that women must fit into other roles can be offensive and upsetting to the audience. Be mindful of your terms and how gender roles can be negated.
- **Employing internationally and racially friendly terminology.** For example, referring to non-white individuals as "people of color" is more proper than other outdated terminology and will undoubtedly help the audience feel respected.
- **Avoid stereotyping the crowd.** Stereotyping can be based on race, age, gender, sexuality, or other identity-related bases, and it is never a good option.

Practice using inclusive language before you go on stage to ensure it flows naturally within your vocabulary—inclusive language should not be jarring!

BODY LANGUAGE

Make sure that you pay special attention to your body language as well. Your body language conveys messages beyond what your mouth says to the audience. Crossed arms and a podium blocking you the whole time make you appear closed off, whereas facing the audience with your arms naturally to your sides says, "I am confident and ready to chat with you," making communication a two-way street.

In order to help the proper body language come naturally to you, make sure that when you rehearse, you do so with the proper stances. Rehearse with a relaxed posture, which includes keeping your arms by your sides or gesturing appropriately. And speaking of, you can further emphasize your speech with subtle gestures. Indeed, touching your heart empathetically during touching moments, for example, can subtly influence the audience into believing your words.

Something that can help you with your body language is practicing the six basic body language movements for a speech, as follows:

1. Posture. Keep a neutral posture with your shoulders back and relaxed, your arms uncrossed and out of your pockets, and your body facing the audience. Your standing posture is like your silent introduction. It communicates volumes about your confidence, credibility, and openness.

a. Sitting Posture. There may be situations where you must speak while seated, such as during a panel discussion or an interview. In such scenarios, maintaining a good sitting posture is crucial. Sit upright with your feet flat on the floor, your back against the chair, and your shoulders relaxed. Lean slightly forward when speaking to show engagement and interest. A good sitting posture can make you appear more professional, confident, and engaged, enhancing the effectiveness of your speech.

2. Breathing. It can be easy for your breathing to become labored on stage; use relaxed breathing to ensure you can project your voice and pause to emphasize significant points.

3. Gestures. Use hand gestures to emphasize and punctuate what you are saying, and use varied gestures to keep your audience's attention. Also, if you change a PowerPoint slide, look at it momentarily! This cues your audience to do the same.

4. The Eyes. The eyes are often referred to as the windows to the soul. In public speaking, eye contact can open a connection window between you and your audience, making your speech more personal, engaging, and impactful. Let's delve deeper into the role of eye contact in effective communication.

a. Eye Contact. Make eye contact by looking from one face to the next and watching the crowd. It's a non-verbal greeting that says, "I see you, I acknowledge you, and I value your presence." It helps establish a personal connection with your audience, making them feel seen and engaged. Just as maintaining eye contact is important, knowing when to break eye contact is equally crucial. Constant, unbroken eye contact can feel intimidating or uncomfortable to your audience.

Eye Contact with Large Audiences. Making eye contact with a large audience can seem daunting. The key is to make each individual feel seen and included. Achieve this by dividing the audience into sections and alternating your gaze between these sections. Look at a person in one section, then shift your gaze to a person in another section. This creates a sense of inclusion and engagement across the entire audience, making your speech more impactful and engaging.

b. Raising Eyebrows. Imagine you're sharing an exciting piece of news with a friend, and their eyebrows shoot up in surprise. This slight movement can convey their surprise more effectively than words. Raising your eyebrows can express surprise, interest, or curiosity in your speaking.

c. Eye Squinting. Squinting is a facial expression often associated with skepticism, disbelief, or deep thought. In speeches, squinting at the right moment can convey to your audience that you're thinking deeply or questioning something.

5. Movement. Make sure to move around in the space you have for your presentation; when used effectively, movement can add dynamism to your speech. Walking across the stage can help you engage with different sections of your audience, while moving toward the audience can create a sense of intimacy and engagement. However, aimless pacing or fidgeting can be distracting and convey nervousness. If you choose to move, do so with purpose and poise.

6. Facial expression. Make sure to smile! Think of a time when you were greeted with a warm, genuine smile. You likely felt a sense of warmth and positivity. A smile is a universal sign of happiness and friendliness. In public speaking, smiling can make you appear more approachable, confident, and enthusiastic.

> **a. Frowning.** A frown can express a range of emotions, from worry and confusion to disagreement and displeasure. In public speaking, frowning can signal to your audience that something is serious, concerning, or deserving of their attention.

When you take the time and patience to build up your communication skills for a speech, you will notice marked improvements in your confidence and your audience's engagement.

ENHANCING YOUR VOICE

In the grand symphony of public speaking, your voice is your most powerful instrument. It can whisper like the breeze, roar like the ocean, or resonate like a drum. Each element plays a unique role in shaping your speech's melody. By understanding and manipulating these elements, you can conduct your symphony with skill and finesse, captivating your audience and making your speech a performance to remember.

Start by focusing on your speed. Chances are, you are more likely to speak far too fast than too slow—which many nervous people suffer from. One way to find a good pace for yourself is to find an excerpt of text of about 150 words. Make sure that it takes you over a minute to recite that passage; this is the speed at which most people can comfortably listen to and retain information.

In addition, the speed at which you speak can influence how your message is received. Speaking quickly can convey excitement, urgency, or passion. Speaking slowly can emphasize important points, create suspense, or give your audience time to absorb complex information. By controlling your speaking speed, you can guide your audience's attention, enhance comprehension, and control the rhythm of your speech.

Next, make sure that your pronunciation is clear as well. Everyone has an accent of some shape or form, and some people mumble when speaking faster or more nervously. As you speak while rehearsing, note any words you tend to smash together or stumble over or where a regional accent takes hold. Then, if you plan to use these words, practice enunciating them more clearly. Furthermore, ensure you can pronounce any technical terms clearly and correctly for the audience.

Now, imagine you're at a coffee shop, overhearing two conversations. At one table, a woman's voice drips with sarcasm as she says, "Nice job, really." At another, a man's voice brims with genuine enthusiasm as he exclaims, "Nice job, really!" The same words but completely different meanings are conveyed through tone.

In public speaking, your tone is the emotional undertone that shapes the meaning of your words. It's the difference between "I'm fine," said with a cheerful tone, and "I'm fine," said with a resigned tone. Your tone can express a range of emotions - from excitement and enthusiasm to seriousness and sorrow. By varying your tone to match your message, you can make your speech more engaging and emotionally resonant.

This leads us to pitch. Have you ever heard the screech of a car's brakes or the deep rumble of thunder? The high pitch of the screech and the low pitch of the thunder are hard to ignore. Pitch, the highness or lowness of a sound, plays a crucial role in public speaking.

A high pitch can convey excitement, urgency, or enthusiasm, while a low pitch can suggest authority, calmness, or seriousness. By varying your pitch, you can emphasize key points, express different emotions, and keep your audience's attention. Just like a song that uses a variety of pitches to create a melody, a speech that uses a variety of pitches can be more engaging and impactful.

Finally, chunking and pausing are some other skills to be mindful of. Remember how I mentioned earlier that you can use timed pauses to emphasize what you are saying? That is true, but it helps a ton if you take the time to chunk what you are saying into logical clusters and *then* pause, emphasizing a group of matching information. Pausing after iterating a point or making a shocking statement works better than in the middle of an explanation.

Using strategic pauses is like using punctuation in writing. Just as a period signals the end of a sentence and prepares the reader for the next one, a pause signals the completion of a thought and prepares your audience for the next one. By mastering the art of strategic pauses, you can enhance your speech's clarity, emphasis, and rhythm.

Try recording yourself as you rehearse to help you understand where there might be room for improvement within your speech. It might feel awkward at first, but by listening to the recording you made, you can find areas of the speech that might be confusing, clunky, or able to be improved upon as you give the speech for real.

Voice modulation is like the paintbrush in the hand of an artist. It allows you to add color, depth, and texture to the canvas of your speech. With the proper techniques, you can train your voice to be more flexible, expressive, and impactful. Let's explore some techniques to help you fine-tune your voice modulation skills and ways to warm up before you go out on stage.

You can do this by practicing a few vocal exercises and running your speech one final time before you go on. If you are interested in vocal exercises to try, consider the following:

- **The nonsense exercise.** For about one minute, pretend you are giving your speech, but speak complete gibberish. Rather than focusing on content, spend this time paying attention to tone, speed, pitch, and other facets of your voice.

- **Singing Exercises.** Singing is a natural way to improve your voice modulation. It helps enhance your vocal range, tone control, and rhythm while warming up your voice. Sing along to a song you like, paying attention to how you modulate your voice to match the melody. Practice different types of songs to challenge your vocal range and control.

- **Tongue Twisters**. Tongue twisters are the verbal equivalent of an obstacle course. They challenge your articulation, speed, and pronunciation, making them an excellent tool for improving your voice modulation. Practice saying tongue twisters slowly at first, focusing on clear articulation. Then, gradually increase your speed while maintaining clarity. This exercise can help improve your pronunciation, speed control, and vocal agility, as well as warm up your voice just before a speech.

- **Read Aloud.** Reading aloud is like a workout for your voice. Choose a piece of text - it could be a book, a newspaper article, or a script - and read it aloud. Pay attention to how you use your voice to convey the meaning of the text.

Focusing on your voice gives you that special something to truly optimize your speech. Dedicate time to these exercises, and watch as your voice transforms from a mere sound into a symphony that captivates your audience and resonates long after the final word has been spoken.

INTERACTIVE ELEMENT: FILLER FREE SPEECH

Instructions

Fillers are the worst nightmare of an audience who came for an eloquent speech. Use the following exercise to help you break free from the clutches of filler words and phrases in just 60 seconds:

1. Choose a simple topic you can speak about for one solid minute. It could be a personal anecdote, a brief hobby description, or a favorite book or movie review.
2. Use a timer or stopwatch to limit yourself to 60 seconds. This constraint will encourage you to be concise.
3. Stand in front of a mirror, maintaining good posture and making eye contact with yourself.
4. Begin talking about your chosen topic. Focus on delivering a clear, coherent message without using any fillers. Speak at a steady pace.
5. Instead of using fillers, practice inserting brief pauses when collecting your thoughts. Pauses are much more effective at maintaining your flow than fillers.
6. As you speak, pay attention to your reflection in the mirror. If you catch yourself using a filler, start the timer over and continue from where you left off.

Perform this exercise multiple times with different topics to build your confidence and improve your ability to speak without fillers. It is also a good idea to record yourself as you do this exercise, as this can allow you to reflect on what the camera sees, not just what you remember. After each practice session, reflect on your progress and identify areas where you tend to use fillers. Focus on improving those areas during your next practice.

Conclusion

Oprah Winfrey said, "[g]reat communication begins with connection." How you communicate with your audience is everything and will help you become more confident and deliver memorable speeches. Speaking of memory, it's time to see how you can engage a room, keep them engaged, and leave a memorable impression.

6

MEMORY: THE BLUEPRINT FOR AN ENGAGED AUDIENCE

D id you know that the average attention span of an audience is only six to eight minutes (31 Fear of Public Speaking Statistics (Prevalence), n.d.)? Capturing an audience's attention can be challenging, whether it's your family, friends, investors, or employer. You need skills to capture and maintain their attention to make an impressionable speech. Therefore, this chapter will help you find your captivating skills, even if you're a nervous speaker.

ELEMENTS OF KEEPING AN AUDIENCE ENGAGED

It's not enough to know how to speak to an audience, you also need to know how to keep them captivated. Therefore, before you can truly master the art of engaging an audience and ensuring your speech remains fresh, let's learn some crucial facts about audience engagement.

Aristotle knew he had to engage an audience to trigger their memory and keep them captivated. This was an idea as plain as day to him—an audience who was not engaged would be unable to pay close attention to the speech, forgetting words as fast as he spoke them. With this comes the knowledge that rehearsal is one of the keys; it prevents you from stumbling as much, making you a more compelling speaker. However, the magic behind captivation does not stop there.

The bottom line is that you cannot keep an audience engaged without first capturing the heart of their attention. How are you meant to do that? Through your introduction, of course! Contrary to popular belief, you can think about your speech's introduction as the *central* part of the speech. During your introduction, you have the floor and the ability to captivate or alienate the audience. It is, therefore, vital to start with something that instantly captures their attention.

Momentum is your best friend for keeping an audience on the edge of their seats. Momentum keeps your speech flowing, allowing your audience's interest to ebb and flow naturally; just when they think you are done, you hit them with another point of interest and begin the process all over. There are many different ways to employ momentum in your speech, but one of the best ways to do so involves humor!

So, to sum up the elements of keeping an audience engaged, you need three key components: capturing their attention, building momentum, and rehearsing. Combined, these three elements show that you are confident and help you engage the audience and maintain their attention. Now that you know what is required, let us see how you can work on developing those skills.

HOW TO KEEP AN AUDIENCE ENGAGED

An unengaged audience is the worst nightmare for a speaker—even the greatest ones. Speaking to an audience who is disinterested, heads lolling back into a light sleep even, can be disheartening. You spent all this time preparing only for the audience to pass out halfway through! How mortifying. Well, let's see how you can keep that audience perfectly engaged so that you don't fall victim to this nightmare coming true.

I have mentioned it before, but your audience will not care about a speech on a topic they are not interested in. Plain and simple. If you have the choice as to what your speech is about, you absolutely cannot skip tailoring it to the audience. Indeed, you have to keep in mind your audience's interests, expertise, and knowledge as you prepare for the speech. Even when you *cannot* pick the speech's topic, you can still tailor it!

Tailoring your speech to the audience does not have to feel like an uphill battle. Just a few ways that you can do so include the following:

- **Define terms.** Provide a definition if there is a term you think the audience might be unfamiliar with, especially if it is technical or scientific. At the same time, do not define basic terms your audience is likely already well-versed in; doing so can seem condescending!

- **Use anecdotes.** Anecdotes are stories that you can pepper throughout your speech. Try infusing your speech with relatable stories and characters that speak to the audience, allowing them to identify with your words.
- **Make statistics matter.** To you, the statistic might make perfect sense in the context of what you are saying. The thing is, your audience may not feel the same. So, use statistics in context, even drawing comparisons between ideas to make those statistics meaningful.

In addition, you can help build engagement and interest in a speech by interacting before the speech starts. Mingle with the audience and initiate small conversations with those in the crowd. Then, when you step out onto the stage, audience members will be drawn to you—saying things like, "Wow, I spoke to that person earlier! Let's see what they have to say!"

Another tip for keeping the audience engaged is using humor. Be yourself when using humor. Even dry humor can work when delivered authentically. Not only does laughter reduce stress, but a joke that lands nicely can captivate the audience and help them relate to you more. At the same time, balance humor with earnest speaking and steer clear of offensive or questionable words or phrases. Again, offending the crowd is *never* the way to go.

You can also make use of shocking or interesting facts in order to get the audience to listen. Within the particular field you are presenting for, whether it's a toast or a product launch, there are bound to be striking facts or news articles you can share. Not only does this direct the audience's attention to you from the first moment, but it can also help contextualize your speech a bit more for the audience.

Moreover, it would be best if you made it a point to include interaction in your speech. Audiences cannot ignore your words if they genuinely feel part of the speech. Mention that a Q&A session will be included, and try to include unique points of audience participation within your speech to make it more exciting for everyone involved.

As much as you can add to a speech to keep the audience engaged, there are also modes of speech that can dissuade an otherwise engaged audience from listening. One of the major culprits of disinterest for an audience is the use of filler words. If you have ever listened to a speaker whose speech was rife with words like "like," "um," "uh," or "you know," then you understand how vital dismantling filler words can be. They don't add anything, and regardless of why you use them, they can sound uneducated, too. So, try to prune these filler words from your speech as much as possible, revisiting Chapter 5's activity to help.

Lastly, try to add key takeaways to your speech before moving into the momentous parts of it. This is especially helpful if you use the teacher approach mentioned earlier. Including key take-aways keeps the content fresh in the minds of the audience members.

BUILDING THE PERFECT MOMENTUM

Now that you have some advice for keeping the audience engaged, you must look at building the perfect momentum. Snowballing the speech from the ground up is the best way to keep it enticing and to build anticipation and excitement for the speech as you go. How exactly can you work to build flawless momentum?

In order to build momentum for your speech, you have first to understand what exactly momentum *is*. Building momentum means using visual or verbal cues to continue guiding your audience throughout your speech. Think about building a snowman; you roll the snow up into a ball, and that ball gets bigger and bigger until boom—you have a finished snowman. A speech is just like that; momentum helps you transition the audience from one topic to another. In essence, momentum is significant because it boosts the speech and supports its transitions.

On that note, your transitions matter significantly. They have to be smooth but noticeable. Transitions should be catchy yet indicate that the topic is gliding elsewhere and should also be used to bridge the content as well. Examples of transitions include:

- **Use visual aids.** For example, do not just rely on a PowerPoint; include charts, physical items, and more. This keeps the audience enticed and helps them understand the flow of the speech far better.

- **Encourage chatter.** Instead of making the audience listen to you the entire time, encourage them to talk with one another and then share ideas. This allows for a break from listening and for more engagement.
- **Use videos.** A short video can break up bigger chunks of your speech and make it more palatable, as well as the inclusion of visual displays of data or actions you describe in your speech.

You can make a stellar speech that snowballs momentum and engagement by rehearsing for proper transitions.

Speaking of snowballs, just like how they build up from small to large, so should your speech. Start with the most minor jokes and topics before steadily building up to more intricate topics and jokes. This gives your audience time to acclimate to the topic and helps them build anticipation as you speak.

If you have not noticed by now, anticipation is vital to building momentum. You can also build anticipation by pausing between transitions and topics. Pausing during a speech is a great way to punctuate statements—*literally*. A pause serves as a vocal punctuation mark to help your listeners complete a thought, meaning pausing between transitions can be great for building momentum to the next central point.

Being yourself is, believe it or not, another spectacular way to build momentum in a speech. No one wants to listen to a speaker who is clearly being inauthentic or pretending to be someone they are not. Because of this, it's essential to be yourself. Think of yourself as a character because, to your audience, you are. So, how would you build your character arc naturally while using the speech as a catalyst?

In order to keep your momentum going and allow the audience to follow along with the brilliant cadences of your speech, you should not fear going off-script. You may plan, rehearse, and re-plan your speech countless times over, but it may surprise you that the off-script moments are what truly catapult your speech into greatness. As such, you should allow yourself to be natural and *improvise* if your speech calls for it in the name of momentum.

As you progress and hope to build up true momentous power throughout your speech, do not forget the power of storytelling. Use storytelling to create an air of personality, as it can infuse your personality as you present your information to the crowd. For example, you could use one narrative that links throughout all your points, ultimately reaching a stunning conclusion. This is just one technique that employs storytelling for momentum success, and I highly advise it.

It also helps keep your speech going if you ask the listeners questions. Your audience might not know what to ask, and they might not know where the speech is headed either. But if you start asking questions, it leaves them in anticipation of an answer. Good questions to include are ones that ask about a solution to a problem, how we know what we know, or the effects that one thing can have on another.

These methods are beautiful ways to build momentum, but what if you want something more subtle? One of the most valuable tactics you can learn is "idea building," where you allow a point, idea, or concept to start small and then build throughout the speech. This is a good momentum tactic because it tricks the audience into feeling like they have played an active part in the development of the speech.

Now, at the end of your speech, what you do with all the momentum you have built up is vital. You cannot just build the audience up only to disappoint them at your conclusion. So, how do you use the momentum wisely? There are a couple of ways in which you can go about this. One of the best ways is with a *call to action*.

A call to action is a statement, often at the end of a work, speech, or persuasive document, that encourages the attendee to take action aligned with the contents of the speech. For example, a call to action about the launch of a new car seat might sound like "the options are clear; there is one brand that will truly harness your baby's safety and comfort for the optimal car ride. Do not let this opportunity pass you by."

However, your call to action does not have to convince someone to buy or do anything. You can encourage them to ask questions, carry a message with them, or otherwise feel compelled by your words. Indeed, a call to action does not have to seem demanding. Whatever you choose to end your speech with, it should be powerful and capitalize on the momentum you built up.

HANDLING CHALLENGES MID-SPEECH

As much as we would like our speeches to go well, with no challenges, that is obviously not always what happens. Sometimes, you will be asked challenging questions that are a trap or that you could not have prepared for; other times, you will walk on stage to a reactive audience—and there's nothing you can do to change that.

When this happens, you might feel discouraged and frankly afraid as you stand in a vulnerable position before an audience. What are you to do in a situation like this? The good news is that there are solutions and ways to navigate this, and I will share those with you now.

Before you launch your speech, ensure the audience knows that questions are welcome. Make them feel comfortable asking you anything, and do so with confidence *and* humility. You might think it is a bad idea to welcome questions right from the start, but you accomplish a few things in doing so. In fact, you:

- Dissuade people from trying to catch you off guard intentionally—because sometimes those rude individuals exist.
- Disarm a reactive audience from thinking you are some overconfident, money-grubbing individual by showing them that you are open and there for *their* benefit.
- Imply that while your speech does its best, nothing is perfect. This keeps audiences light on you while demonstrating that you anticipate questions, thus making you a more credible speaker.

So, despite what you might have thought beforehand, inviting questions at the start of a speech is a good practice.

Naturally, because you are inviting the audience to ask questions about the contents of your speech, you should also anticipate those questions. Consider the audience and their background as you review your main points, visual aids, and other components of your speech. If you were sitting in that crowd and came from the same background, what questions might you ask a speaker? Anticipating these questions and preplanning your answers is one magnificent way to avoid stumbling on stage.

It is also a good idea to try to view incoming questions positively. When someone asks you a question, it provides ways to improve your speech moving forward. If you have to repeat the speech later on, you can include those answers in your speech; if not, you know what kinds of questions to anticipate being asked in the future.

Of course, the most concerning parts of your speech—the ones that genuinely unnerve you or trip you up—may not even come from questions. Maybe they come from the audience instead; after all, we are not always fortunate enough to have a respectful and receptive audience. When you have an audience that is aggravated, unnerving, unwilling to listen, or just plain reactive to everything that seems to come out of your mouth, a few tactics can make the speech easier for you.

For example, it's a good idea to make sure that you maintain eye contact with the audience. I have mentioned it before, but it is imperative to maintain eye contact with a resistant crowd-think high school assemblies! It is not about eye contact itself; instead, these types of audiences focus on your *lack* of eye contact, as not making eye contact can expose you as a feeble speaker.

It is also wise to, if your audience asks a question, truly ensure that you understand their question or point. Remember: *You can ask questions even though you are the speaker!* Before launching into a passionate answer, ensure you know what needs to be answered; otherwise, you risk making a fool of yourself in front of a potentially unforgiving audience.

Furthermore, if your audience asks you something or interjects, take the time to validate what they have said. Many speakers can seem dismissive when they answer questions or reply to comments; avoid doing this to extend respect to the audience and heighten your credibility.

I want to ensure you are more prepared than ever when handling these mid-speech challenges, showing the audience and yourself that you mean business. In addition to the above, do your best to remain calm. The audience can tell if you are becoming riled up; if they are there to taunt or aggravate you, they will use that to their advantage.

Moreover, keep in mind that you can be *honest*. If you aren't sure of an answer, strive to be honest with your audience. Let them know you are unsure of the answer but will undoubtedly put in time to expand your knowledge. And, of course, make sure that they know you genuinely appreciate the question. This prevents hostility while showing that it is okay for you not to know everything and prevents the spread of misinformation.

Now, whatever you do, avoid making attacks, whether directly or passively, on the audience. Even if you have the rudest audience in the world, responding with rudeness wipes your credibility as a speaker away. Beyond that, it turns any neutral or positive parties against you and may even prevent you from being asked to speak again.

I also recommend checking in with the audience throughout the speech. An audience is more likely to become volatile if they remain confused for large portions of the speech. As such, instead of allowing this confusion to fester, ask the audience if they have any questions throughout the speech—and again, be receptive to those questions as well.

Lastly, try your best to end the speech positively, even if the course of the speech was not the best. More so, this means that you should not end on a negative note. The last few moments of your speech are what is going to stick in the mind of the audience. Ending on a positive note proves that you are a good speaker; on the other hand, letting yourself become pessimistic toward the end invites them to negate everything you said!

INTERACTIVE ELEMENT: 10-MINUTE MOMENTUM BUILDER

Instructions

In just ten minutes a week, you can master the process of building momentum into a speech. Here is how:

1. Find a quiet and comfortable space where you will not be interrupted and clear your mind. Set a timer for ten minutes before you begin. You will mock-draft a speech, helping you build confidence in your momentum mastery.

2. Pick a topic that interests you and fits the context of a short speech. This can be anything from a hobby to a topic you are learning about.

3. In one minute, write down the opening of your speech. This should be an attention-grabbing statement or a thought-provoking question related to your topic.

4. In the following minute, write a brief introduction that provides context for your topic. Explain why it is relevant or important.

5. In the minute after that, list the main points or key ideas you want to cover in your speech. These are the building blocks of your speech.

6. In the next two minutes, jot down a sentence or two for each main point, briefly explaining or expanding on them. Write a transition sentence that connects your introduction to your first main point smoothly.

7. Finish by writing a concluding sentence that connects your main points and leaves a memorable impression.

8. With five minutes remaining, start speaking your speech out loud. Focus on articulation, clarity, and maintaining a steady pace.

9. Within the speech, practice building momentum. Focus on transitioning from your first main point to the second, starting from the introduction and building

momentum as you go, culminating with your conclusion.

10. After the timer goes off, take a moment to reflect on your practice. What went well, and what could be improved?

If it takes more than ten minutes your first time around, don't sweat it; keep practicing until you master this skill!

Conclusion

Leslie Stephen said, "[t]he only way in which one human being can properly attempt to influence another is by encouraging him to think for himself; instead of endeavoring to instill ready-made opinions into his head."

You cannot maintain your audience's attention entirely without getting them involved, building momentum, and captivating them with incredible stories, facts, or visual aids. Try practicing the methods you discovered in this chapter, and once you're feeling confident, it will be time to move on to the final stage before everything comes together: delivery.

7

DELIVERY: THE ART OF MASTERING PERSUASION WITH NLP

D iscover the secrets to engaging your audience, influencing their thoughts and actions, and delivering a speech that leaves a lasting impact. In this chapter, you will learn how to connect with your audience by addressing their fears and using simple tactics to persuade them. And that's not all – you will also master Aristotle's final framework element: delivery. With powerful diction, psychology, and clever tricks, you will learn how to deliver your speech with confidence, even if you start off feeling nervous. Let's take your public speaking skills to the next level.

ALL ABOUT DICTION

Even the most captivating speech can sound monotonous if delivered without passion. Why is that? It is because of *diction*— the words you say and *how* you say them. Make no mistake, these play a huge role in what your audience takes away from your speech. It is like cooking—if you set the finest ingredients in front of someone who could burn water, they will not become a master chef, will they?

Because of this, looking at how you deliver a speech with confidence is vital. Aristotle devised that delivery was the final canon of rhetoric in making a speech go from okay to extraordinary, and now we will explore just that. You will find influence and persuasion over your audience through these methods that allow you to command your diction like an expert.

Now, it seems simple enough, but what does delivery really entail? At a glance, your delivery of a speech is going to involve body language, tone, and diction. This means that what you say and how you say it matters equally as much as how you command your body. In previous chapters, you mastered tone and body language; now, it is time to take a look at that skill of diction for flawless delivery.

You might recognize the word "diction" from your high school English classes back in the day, but if not, that is okay! Defined, diction refers to the choices you make in a speech to convey something. For example, you can say, "The plane flew over the school," but that exact phrase with better diction would be something like, "A mammoth of a plane soared unforgivingly above the school." In the latter phrasing, so many implications about size, shape, and even pilot skill are added—all thanks to diction.

This leads us to how diction can help your speech. Beyond providing a more vivid picture for the audience, what are the benefits of speaking with good diction? Well, some of those benefits include the following:

- **A tone that supports your purpose.** Diction contributes massively to the tone of a speech. Using diction alone, you can transfer the context of a speech from a casual conversation to a scientific report. Thus, diction is also crucial because it helps ensure that your speech is appropriate to the context.
- **Support of the setting.** Diction benefits the storytelling of your speech, helps you foster credibility, and more "setting"-based influences as well. When you make strong diction choices, you do not have to worry about whether the audience has enough context.
- **Establishment of a narrative voice.** Diction helps you establish a central voice for the story you are telling across the narrative arc of your speech. This helps the audience view you consistently, positively, and credible as you present.

As you can see, diction is an invaluable tool to take a speech to the next level, commanding persuasion and confidence.

Something that many people are unaware of is that there are actually *eight* different types of diction. This means you have eight different diction types to choose from when considering how you elevate your speech. Those eight types of diction are as follows:

1. **Formal diction.** Formal diction involves the use of elevated or sophisticated language. You will not speak with slang riddling your language if you need to use formal diction. Furthermore, syntax—the structure in which your sentences take shape—tends to be far more complicated in formal diction contexts. Formal diction is usually best suited for professional or legal matters.

2. **Informal diction.** Informal diction often takes a more conversational shape. It's the language used in fiction stories or general communication which boils down to the fact that we typically use informal diction within everyday life. Informal diction is often prized for its ability to offer a heightened level of freedom for writers and speakers alike, which means that your wedding toasts or casual speeches might benefit from a more informal air.

3. **Pedantic diction.** Pedantic diction involves being highly academic or detailed within your language choices. Usually, someone who uses pedantic diction explicitly picks most words by hand, carefully crafting each word to hold ample meaning for the work. Naturally, this style lends itself best to more formal writing and speeches.

4. **Colloquial diction.** Colloquial diction employs colloquialisms like regional slang and diction to add vibrancy and dimension to a work. It adds culture in certain respects, but do not force colloquial diction into your speech if it does not flow naturally.

5. **Slang diction.** As the name would suggest, slang diction employs slang terms within it. This is usually done to

loosen formalities if it fits naturally into your authentic voice and you are trying to connect with the audience.

6. **Abstract diction.** Abstract diction occurs when you use more abstract phrases to describe a point. It is not the same as a colorful metaphor; abstract diction is vaguer and not necessarily as logical. Abstract diction can be used effectively in certain types of speeches.

7. **Concrete diction.** Concrete diction uses words in their most literal sense and often uses language that appeals to the five senses. This can help speeches be interpreted more literally and without open interpretation due to the detailed yet specific nature of the word choice.

8. **Poetic diction.** Poetic diction involves lyrical words that reflect a central theme, and although this form of diction is commonly used in poetry or literature alone, you can find specific spaces for it in a speech.

The diction that you will want to use for your speech depends on the purpose, audience, and context. You can even blend different forms of diction for a perfect, idiosyncratic tone for your speech.

Introducing... Neurolinguistic Programming!

Now, it is time to discuss something called neurolinguistic programming. Also referred to as NLP, neurolinguistic programming can be a valuable tool and skill in the context of a speech. You are probably wondering what neurolinguistic programming is and how it can relate to diction, so allow me to clarify that now.

Neurolinguistic programming is a pseudoscientific approach to communication, personal development, and psychotherapy. The theory of NLP is that there is a connection between neurological processes, language, and behavioral patterns learned through experience, which can be changed to achieve specific goals in life.

Neurolinguistic Programming can enhance communication and engagement in your speeches. Let's review how NLP principles apply to public speaking:

1. **Rapport Building:** NLP emphasizes the importance of connecting with the audience. You can use techniques such as mirroring body language, tone, and tempo to create a sense of empathy and connection with the audience.
2. **Sensory Acuity:** You should be acutely aware of your audience's reactions to your speech. By paying close attention to non-verbal cues such as facial expressions, gestures, and postures, you can gauge your audience's engagement levels and then adjust your speech, speed, volume, tone, or even style to keep the audience engaged.
3. **Representational Systems:** Individuals perceive the world using their primary sensory systems- Visual, Auditory, Kinesthetic, Olfactory, and Gustatory (VAKOG). Your speeches should incorporate language that appeals to all these senses to make them more vivid and memorable. For instance, you can use visual

language to create an image, auditory language to evoke sounds, and kinesthetic language to express emotions.

4. **Anchoring:** This NLP technique creates a stimulus-response pattern that can be triggered at will. For example, you might use a specific gesture, a physical location on the stage, or a phrase to anchor certain emotions in the audience, such as enthusiasm or calmness, to support your message.

5. **Meta-Model:** NLP's meta-model is a tool for understanding and clarifying language. You should use it to craft clear, concise, and specific messages, reducing ambiguity and increasing the impact of your speech. For example, let's imagine you have received a question from the audience. The meta-model involves asking targeted questions to uncover specifics hidden by deletions (missing information), generalizations (broad, sweeping statements), and distortions (assumptions presented as facts); it encourages precise speech. For instance, if someone says, "I'm stuck," asking, "How exactly are you stuck?" can lead to a more productive conversation.

6. **Milton Model:** Unlike the Meta-Model, the Milton Model uses deliberately vague and metaphorical language to allow listeners to fill in the gaps with their own experiences and interpretations, making the speech more relatable and persuasive. You can use this in your speeches to weave stories and suggest ideas that resonate on a personal level with your audience, allowing for a more inclusive and engaging experience.

7. **Reframing:** This is about changing the frame of reference for a particular situation or statement to give it a different meaning. In your speech, this can be useful in overcoming objections, presenting alternative perspectives, or turning challenges into opportunities by simply reframing them into something positive or neutral.

8. **Pattern Interrupt:** This technique breaks the audience's expectation pattern, regains their attention, or changes the interaction's direction. To use this technique, you might use humor, silence, or a thought-provoking statement as a pattern interrupt. Alternatively, if you see your audience drifting, pause and clap your hands really loud. All eyes will be back on you!

9. **Embedded Commands:** These are indirect commands placed within a longer sentence, designed to bypass the conscious mind and speak directly to the subconscious. They can subtly direct the audience toward a desired action or response. For example, "As you begin to relax, notice how you can 'let go' of tension" embeds the command "let go" within a soothing message. When giving speeches, using embedded commands can subtly direct the audience towards desired actions or emotions. It's effective for speakers to highlight their key points by using a distinct tone, pause, or gesture, thereby signaling the subconscious to pay attention to specific phrases without making the command overt.

10. **Storytelling:** Stories can be a powerful way to convey a message. Stories structured with the techniques above

can be used to resonate with the audience's values and beliefs, making your points more persuasive.

There are enough nuances, details, and sub-topics that entire books are written on NLP. Here, I wanted to introduce the topic and highlight key concepts you can start bringing into your speeches today. Some people believe that NLP as a method is quite manipulative. The tool of NLP itself is not a manipulation tactic. When it comes down to it, the intended use determines if it is manipulation.

When you employ neurolinguistic programming in your speech, be sure of your intention. While it can certainly be a powerful tool, in the wrong hands, NLP can be a very negative thing. With this book, I aim to focus on the positive usage of such a tool.

THE POWER OF NEUROLINGUISTIC PROGRAMMING

With those basics of NLP established, it is time to explore how to use NLP to build connection and confidence.

Mirroring

One of the most popular and effective neurolinguistic programming tactics is "mirroring." Mirroring is a powerful tool to help you build rapport with your audience. This skill primarily applies to body language, so it is particularly effective for speeches in front of smaller or more intimate crowds. Still, let's go over how you can employ mirroring, and then you can decide whether it fits within the context of your speech or not.

Fortunately, the mirroring technique is among the easiest to master. It is said that the vast majority of communication is relayed through body language, which means that it is undoubtedly a good thing that such an easy technique stems from body language. With this technique, you will mirror your body language to meet that of the audience.

Of course, it's not easy to mirror an entire crowd simultaneously, which is why I said this works best for more intimate groups. However, you might mirror a few key individuals' body language, which can work. For instance, you could mirror your boss or a particularly influential audience member. Some ideas for speaking with mirroring include the following:

- If they lean in, you lean in too.
- Match what they are doing with their arms or legs.
- If they nod their head, follow that movement and nod with them.

If an audience member or two gets the chance to speak to you during your speech, you can also mirror how they speak; following their speech with a parallel structure is an excellent way to go.

In public speaking, mirroring shows that you are in sync with the audience and understand and empathize with their reactions. However, taken to the extreme, it can be overdone. So, balance it with your natural body movements.

Modeling

Modeling is another successful NLP technique that you can employ to your benefit. It is one of the most successful NLP methods for entrepreneurs and others to gain success and confidence.

Modeling in neurolinguistic programming is the process of replicating the skills of exceptional speakers. It involves observing and mapping the successful behaviors, thought patterns, and beliefs of those who excel in a particular field or activity to learn how they achieve their results. The goal is to create a "model" that you can use to accomplish similar outcomes.

So, to properly engage with modeling, I recommend finding speakers—either in-person or online—whose style of speaking you love. Study their style, including verbal and nonverbal communication. Study how they move and how they stand. Their body language. Their speech patterns and choice of words. And note anything else you would like to emulate. Then, bring your notes into your practice. As you focus on improvement, you will attract that improvement to yourself thanks to modeling your work after what you thought was successful in others.

Modeling is one of the foundational techniques of NLP because it is based on the premise that if one person can do something well, you can, too, through effective modeling.

Imagery Training

Imagery training is another skill that coincides with neurolinguistic programming. This is more of a rehearsal technique than a technique you will use with a crowd, but what you practice during rehearsal certainly shows during your speech in front of a crowd. Also called "mental rehearsal," imagery training posits itself as one of the most essential NLP skills because of how effective it is.

As we briefly considered earlier in the book, the brain struggles to distinguish a strong visualization from reality. Because imagery training relies on visualization, you effectively train your brain to experience reality in a new light. It sounds far-fetched, but it is relatively simple.

You will visualize yourself on stage giving your speech, and that visualization will radiate perfect success. This is going to convince you and your mind that you *are* a successful speaker, already embodying everything it takes to be that vision of success. Moreover, during this visualization, you will want to envision your body language—language that communicates confidence and assuredness.

From there, you will also want to envision clear communication and receptiveness of the crowd. Even running the speech through your head is an excellent idea, which can further enhance the visualization. The more you practice this, the more your confidence will rise.

Neurolinguistic Programming Incantations

The next skill I have to share with you comes in the form of NLP incantations—which, contrary to their name, have nothing to do with magic (although this method works *like* magic!). Incantations were born from affirmations—positive statements that encourage assurance and confidence in various areas of our lives.

Incantations take affirmations to the next level, working to change both your mind and your body to enable a sense of confidence. You must embody what you are trying to say with your whole self, reprogramming your mind for powerful beliefs. This involves combining affirmation-like thoughts with putting yourself in an aligned position, such as affirming success during rehearsal.

More on this in the interactive element at the end of the chapter!

NLP and Thought Leadership

Neurolinguistic programming is believed to enhance one's confidence by improving their "thought leadership" abilities. Thought leadership involves expressing ideas that show your credibility within a given field. This is something that many academics, entrepreneurs, and science-based employees prize themselves on and strive for, and naturally, thought leadership can build your credibility in a speech setting.

The idea of thought leadership is that you are a leader in *thinking* about a particular subject. Who is to say, then, that you cannot be a thought leader in the particular field in which you are presenting? No one! You can become a thought leader and exude credibility by embodying your confidence through NLP methods.

At the same time, trying to use thought leadership means focusing on your experience. Seriously—thought leadership relies heavily on building trust and rapport with an audience, which means you must draw on experience. You *cannot* be a leader in an area where you are inexperienced. That said, drawing on thought leadership ideas is perfect if you present in an area where you have personal, professional, or academic experience.

All in all, these NLP techniques will make you a more compelling speaker. From the words you say to how you pose your body, the audience will pick up on even the most subtle cues you emit. This means that you can intentionally set yourself up for success through the use of NLP tactics. Now, let's move on to where NLP and diction intersect, as this is where you can make even more successful strides!

USING NEUROLINGUISTIC PROGRAMMING FOR PERSUASION

Okay, first off, let us draw our focus back to the connection between neurolinguistic programming and diction for a minute. The words you pick and how you employ them can coincide significantly with the NLP tactics you learned in the last section. So now, we must focus on how you can use them to entice your audience to listen to you as you speak.

One method you can use is to appeal to all five senses in the speech. By this, I mean you can use language that indicates or influences the senses. So, rather than describing the aroma of a candle as "pumpkin"-scented, for instance, you can bump up the imagery and describe it as a "light but creamy pumpkin scent with notes of cinnamon and vanilla intertwined." The latter paints a more resilient picture of how the candle smells while appealing to other senses.

It's also a good idea to use words that evoke strong emotional responses to employ NLP strategies alongside diction further. For example, keeping with the candle, we can add on by saying that the scent is "dreamy and ideal for cherishing the fall season," which paints the picture of fall as something joyous and even adds hints of family involvement (something many people cherish, of course). You can do the same as you describe various concepts in your speech.

In order to pick persuasive words that hit the mark for strong diction, you must first know how to identify a strong word. You can generally tell when a word is strong by how unique it is, how descriptive it is in nature, how action-oriented, or even how surprising it is. These strong words are the opportunity to shock your audience into paying attention, no matter their attention span. Moreover, it's important to note that words elicit particular emotions; use them to build a connection with your audience.

Diction also involves using powerful words and phrases to introduce your topics. Even if your topics are full of stellar word choices, it can kill the flow of your speech if those transitions or introductory phrases are dull or aimless. Some good ways to introduce a topic include a rhetorical question or outstanding statement, for instance. Now, good rhetorical questions are going to be ones that propose a benefit at the same time, like "Are you ready to unleash a new life empowered by self-care?"

You must also walk into your speech armed with powerful words and phrases that help you make a *point*. Sure, your speech and its various points should be strong enough to stand alone, but even the strongest speech must fight against the eight-minute attention span. The words and phrases you unleash into your speech make a difference in how easy it is for your audience to pay attention. Good ways to model that you are reiterating, expounding upon, or hammering in a point include words like "therefore" or "in other words."

At the same time, the words you use to support your points must also be strong. It is not enough to introduce the speech strongly and passionately; that passion has to extend throughout other parts of the speech, too. In order to manage this, you should infuse your vocabulary with phrases like "for example" or "it is evident that." Also, you should not recycle the exact two or three phrases over again. After being used once or twice, a phrase lulls into the back of the audience's mind; therefore, you should come to bat with a handful of phrases you like.

Carefully choose your "unique transition phrases." For example:

- "With this in mind..."
- "Let's pivot to the idea that..."
- "Now, consider the flip side..."
- "As a result..."
- "To illustrate..."

Powerful terms and words must entangle themselves throughout the speech, so it's crucial to have powerful words to end your speech. We will dive into more detail surrounding the conclusion of your speech in Chapter 8, but for now, let's focus on those terms. You should try to spice up your ending phrases a bit. "In conclusion" works, but you can also try things like "If you want to see similar results, then you have to try it yourself." This also doubles as a call to action to inspire the audience.

When all's said and done, it's essential to make sure that you combine neurolinguistic programming alongside strong diction in order to make a lasting impact on the crowd. Remember that your diction should fit your purpose and intent, and simultaneously, it should be appropriate for the context in which you are speaking.

INTERACTIVE ELEMENT: USING NLP

Instructions

Now that you have learned the ins and outs of neurolinguistic programming, let us take a look at a simple activity that can help you master those skills:

1. Locate a quiet space where you can stand in front of a full-length mirror. This exercise is most effective when you can see your entire body.
2. Close your eyes for a moment and visualize yourself speaking confidently in front of an engaged and supportive audience. Imagine yourself standing tall, speaking clearly, and radiating confidence. This sets a positive mental framework.
3. Open your eyes and stand in a "power stance." This involves standing up straight with your shoulders back, feet shoulder-width apart, and your hands on your hips. This posture not only conveys confidence but also boosts it.
4. While maintaining the power stance, look at yourself in the mirror and repeat positive affirmations about your speaking skills. For example, say, "I am a confident speaker who commands the stage. I connect with my audience, and I deliver speeches everyone remembers." Repeat these affirmations several times.
5. Continue to stand in your power stance and practice deep breathing. Inhale deeply through your nose,

expand your diaphragm, and exhale slowly through your mouth. This calms your nerves and improves vocal control.

6. Close your eyes briefly and visualize a supportive and engaged audience. See their smiling faces and feel the positive energy in the room. This creates a mental image of a receptive audience.

7. Open your eyes and, while maintaining the power stance, practice the opening lines of a speech or presentation you would like to improve. Enunciate clearly and confidently.

8. Close your eyes and visualize receiving positive feedback from your audience. Imagine hearing their applause and cheers, seeing them nodding in agreement, and feeling their handshakes as they congratulate you with praise. This reinforces positive outcomes in your mind.

9. Open your eyes, return to a neutral stance, and take a moment to reflect on the confidence you have cultivated in this exercise. Let the confidence soak into you.

10. Close the exercise by affirming that you are better prepared to speak confidently. Believe in the positive changes you have created through this practice.

11. Repeat often!

Conclusion

Benjamin Franklin said, "[i]f you would persuade, you must appeal to interest rather than intellect." Interests and building connections will help you persuade people better than trying to force your expertise or opinions on others who have their own. Once you know how to use the techniques in this chapter, you can move on to the final stage: outlining a speech, which finally shows you how to end one properly!

8

ARISTOTLE'S STEPS TO SPEECH MASTERY: BRINGING IT ALL TOGETHER

This final chapter outlines how to tactically create your speech by walking through Aristotle's wisdom and bringing full circle the eight steps in Chapter 4, which will now include the ending of your speech. In this chapter, I have provided an outline that aims to inspire you to plan every part of your speech by following the necessary steps and considering the advice, rehearsals, and exercises you learned from each of Aristotle's main secrets.

STEP #1: WHO IS YOUR AUDIENCE

Let us revisit and add to some of what you mastered earlier in the book. As you embark upon this first step in outlining your speech, the brunt of your focus needs to be on the audience and what they need at that particular occasion. You don't want to walk on stage with a toast when you are supposed to be presenting your quarterly findings for a company, after all.

As mentioned earlier, you need to truly take the time to analyze your audience. Understanding their background and needs—among other things—will allow you to perfectly refine your speech toward what they need from you, making for a perfect speech that easily captivates everyone.

At the same time, there will be some expectations that you need to check throughout the speech planning period. Ensure you aren't starting with unreasonable expectations for your audience. Things you should consider while planning your speech include:

- Who is your audience, and why are they here?
- How much does your particular audience know about the topic?
- Whether any relevant social or cultural backgrounds play a role in the audience's reception.
- How would that audience usually respond to a similar topic?
- What would be inappropriate in this particular context?

Ensuring that you keep the audience and their needs in mind from the very inception of your speech is the best way to go.

STEP #2: SELECT YOUR TOPIC OR PURPOSE

You will not always be told what you have to present on specifically; sometimes, you are only told that you have to make a speech. The responsibility then falls to you to pick a relevant topic or purpose that the audience will enjoy and remain enthralled by. A general rule is that you should be able to condense your topic into one sentence—usually called a "topic sentence."

In forming your topic or purpose for the speech, you should also try to form a thesis statement. A thesis statement generally follows the format of "[topic statement] is true because of A, B, and C." This aligns perfectly with what we discussed earlier, with a good speech typically having around three main points. You don't have to explicitly state your thesis statement while on stage, but having one ready keeps your thoughts and plan for the speech nice and organized.

Remember, avoid opting for a speech on a topic you aren't familiar with. Even if you do the research, lacking personal experience is something that the audience will be able to pick up on. Therefore, try to pick a good topic that you know well.

You should also ensure that you find the topic at least *somewhat* interesting. While it is of utmost importance that your audience enjoys the topic, it can be a harrowing experience to present on a subject in which you have zero interest. Trust me, you can only fake it for so long! So, ensure you care about the topic at least a little.

STEP #3: GATHER YOUR SPEECH CONTENT (RESEARCH)

The next step involves gathering the contents of your speech. This mainly refers to the body of your speech—the three or so main components you must expand upon between the windows of the introduction and conclusion. Generally, you are going to want your speech to follow an outline such as this:

- Introduction
- Main point 1

  o Evidence 1, 2, 3
  o Addressing potential counterarguments

- Main point 2

  o Evidence 1, 2, 3
  o Addressing potential counterarguments

- Main point 3

  o Evidence 1, 2, 3
  o Addressing potential counterarguments

- Conclusion

Your speech outline can be as long or as brief as you would like, but it should not contain everything you want to say. I recommend always writing your speech in bullet points and avoiding complete sentences. You can confine yourself to six or seven words per bullet or two sentences per main point to help you out with the length of the outline.

This is also the point in your planning process where you should find room for audience engagement—if you plan to have any, that is. You don't want to overload your audience with transitions and engagement, so plan wisely and determine where each engagement instance would occur.

STEP #4: ORGANIZE YOUR SPEECH

Okay, so you might wonder how this differs from Step 3. While step 3 focused on gathering the content, akin to pouring a puzzle out on the table before putting it together, this step involves putting it together! Organizing your speech is what really gives it that extra kick, enabling you to be perfectly prepared along the way.

Now, during your organizational period, it's a good idea to pick a few transitional segues that you can use in your speech. You don't have to memorize them word for word, but you can outline whether you want to use a joke, anecdote, visual aid, or something else to guide the speech along to the next point. This saves you time and stress later, so you don't have to worry about transitions at the drop of a hat.

You can use a few different organizational techniques to better structure not just the overall flow of the speech but the structure of each point as well. Consider those below, for example:

- **Cause and effect.** You can structure it logically by explaining how one cause leads to an effect that's relevant to the point of the speech.
- **Problem and solution.** Another format for your speech points is presenting a problem and then providing its solution.
- **Time.** If you find that you can logically plan your speech in order of time, that can be another excellent option for organizing!
- **Pros and cons.** Ensure that you include pros and cons, which can become the entire layout of your speech—if it makes sense to do so.
- **Steps.** Simply put, you can also use a step-by-step format to organize your speech.

Beyond that, make sure that you have subpoints for each of your main points. You can go on all day about the speech's main points, but without subpoints to truly flesh out the contents, your audience will get bored fast.

STEP #5: OUTLINE THE INTRODUCTION

No, the steps are not in the wrong order—you should *really* outline the introduction *after* you outline the body of your speech! When you work on the introduction later, you have the foresight of having planned the body of your speech in mind. This helps you flawlessly fine-tune the contents of your speech.

Much like the body of a speech, there is an outline you can (and should try to) follow for the introduction of your speech. This is as follows:

- **An attention-getter.** This should be the very first thing that you say—something so compelling that the audience cannot help but listen.
- **A hook.** This is where you introduce yourself and your topic in a smooth and catchy manner. You could use a powerful quote; quotes are like concentrated drops of wisdom. They can express profound truths, evoke deep emotions, and provoke thought. Alternatively, start with a provocative question; questions stimulate curiosity. They engage the mind, making us think and wonder. Opening your speech with a provocative question lets you instantly engage your audience's attention and pique their curiosity. Otherwise, start with a shocking statistic; when used effectively, statistics can be eye-opening. They provide concrete, quantifiable information that can surprise, alarm, or intrigue your audience. Opening your speech with a shocking statistic can grab your audience's attention and highlight the significance of your topic.
- **Your purpose.** Whether subtly or explicitly, you should make a statement that outlines the central point of the speech. What is the purpose of you being here today?
- **Main points.** Make sure to provide a brief outline of your main points!
- **Transition.** Then, you get to transition into the heart of your speech.

It might seem like a lot, but this all happens quickly when you are on stage, getting underway with your speech. You can get as creative as you would like, but the point is that these are, without a doubt, the essential points of any captivating and functional introduction.

STEP #6: PLAN YOUR VISUAL AIDS

The next step that you have to take is planning your visual aids. This is one of the last steps in the process because, ultimately, your visual aids support the rest of your speech. Once you have everything planned up until the end, you can more sufficiently decide what visual aids to use and *where* they should be used throughout the speech.

Refer back to the interactive element at the end of chapter #4 to build an engaging visual!

STEP #7: PLAN PHRASING, TONE, AND BODY LANGUAGE

Next up, you are going to plan the phrasing, tone, and body language of your speech. This naturally comes quite near the end of the process because you have to build your tone and body language around the contents of your speech. You do not want to plan out every little gesture, of course, but taking the time to make plans for major points of your language will certainly be helpful. With your style chosen, it's time to start bringing in the different elements of NLP. Which ones fit the type of speech you are delivering? Which ones will help you engage and connect with the audience?

STEP #8: THE CONCLUSION

Now is when you need to plan the conclusion of your speech for a memorable and impressionable finale, tying everything together succinctly. A great conclusion comes along with four key steps:

1. **A summary.** In order to keep your points fresh in the audience's minds, your conclusion should contain a brief summary of each of the key points of your speech. The human brain is wired to remember the first and last things it encounters; psychologists call this the serial position effect. As your speech draws to a close, your audience is likely to remember your final words. Therefore, it's crucial to summarize your key points.
2. **A thesis.** You should also make it a point to restate the thesis or central idea of your speech. When your audience members leave and get asked what they heard about, they will have your memorable thesis ready to recite!
3. **Benefits.** Mention again how what you have covered benefits the audience, further incentivizing their remembrance.
4. **A clincher or call to action.** Finish with a bang— a call to action is a powerful conclusion tool. It's an invitation to your audience to take a specific action based on your

speech. It could be to adopt a new perspective, make a change in their lives, or even ponder a thought. The call to action serves two purposes. First, it gives your audience a tangible way to respond to your speech. Second, it extends the impact of your speech beyond the event!

Your conclusion cannot be an afterthought or something you create quickly at the very end. Your conclusion is the last thing your audience will hear from you. It must be powerful and leave an impression if your goal is to deliver a speech everyone remembers.

STEP #9: REHEARSE, REHEARSE, REHEARSE!

The last critical step to delivering a great speech, which is mentioned the most in this book, is to rehearse that speech *tirelessly*. And then, just when you think you have rehearsed the speech enough, rehearse it *once more*. Indeed, a good speech is built on the foundation of dedicated rehearsal, which is why this is the final and perhaps most crucial step of the process. Make use of the activities and advice throughout the book to help you get the most from that rehearsal time!

Finally, know there is no shame in keeping some note cards on hand to keep you on track. While burying your head in note cards throughout the entire speech should be avoided, having cue cards to hold onto gives you something to anchor yourself with so that you don't fall too far off course as you improvise on stage.

Conclusion

Colin Powel said, "[t]here are no secrets to success. It is the result of preparation, hard work, and learning from failure." Preparation and hard work always pay off in speaking. Work through these nine steps. Do not rush. Work through each step and review the concepts presented in this book. As General Powel said, your success will result from your preparation and hard work!

SHARE THE MESSAGE

My dream is for you to close this book and immediately plan all the elements of your next public speech. It inspires me to imagine you organizing your talk, working on style and delivery, and crafting a story that will keep your audience curious, engaged, and open to your message.

I hope you can share your own enthusiasm with other readers, by letting them know that this book can help them become the kind of communicators that audiences look forward to listening to.

IN UNDER 1 MINUTE
YOU CAN HELP OTHERS JUST
LIKE YOU BY LEAVING A REVIEW!

Thank you for being part of a community that values the power of connection.

Here's to many public speaking adventures and to the sharing of vital information that can make so many lives better!

Scan the QR code for a quick review!

CONCLUSION

Reflecting on the key lessons and strategies we have explored is important as we navigate to the end of our shared journey. We have delved into the nuances of public speaking, from overcoming fear and embracing self-belief to fine-tuning your delivery and connecting with your audience. Each chapter has armed you with practical strategies to mold you into a confident and effective speaker.

Remember, the journey of mastering public speaking doesn't end here. Mastering it demands continuous improvement and practice. It is a journey that evolves with every speech you deliver and each audience you engage.

The tools and strategies in this book are stepping stones on your path to becoming a compelling speaker. Throughout this guide, we touched on:

- How public speaking sets impressions—the basics of public speaking and why public speaking serves such a pivotal role within our society.
- How to crush social anxiety—tangible methods to fight off the social anxiety roadblock that prevents so many from making compelling speeches.
- Mastering self-confidence—everything you need to unleash radiant self-confidence to overcome doubt and hesitation at any stage.
- The ins and outs of arrangement—how to prepare the speech of your dreams with luxury and ease, concluding in a step-by-step guide.
- Your personal style—making your mark on the audience by embodying your speech methods.
- The essentials of memory—what you need to do to make your audience remember what you said and the key points of your speech.
- Delivering your speech like a pro—thanks to the power of Aristotle's final canon of rhetoric!

But now, the future is in your hands. I wish you the best on your journey forward. I am confident that you have everything you need to succeed. Just use these tools and keep practicing on your public speaking journey, and soon you will have mastered these powerful strategies and be…

… commanding the stage, speaking confidently, and delivering the speech EVERYONE remembers!

REFERENCES

Bernard, M. (2023, July 25). *Speaking clearly for presentations.* Students. https://students.unimelb.edu.au/academic-skills/resources/speaking-and-presenting/speaking-clearly-for-presentations#:

Blanda, S. (2013, April 23). *The introversion bubble.* I. M. H. O. https://medium.com/i-m-h-o/the-introversion-bubble-7d9a96581949#:

Calm Public Speaking Nerves: Let's talk about self-talk. (n.d.). Buckley School of Public Speaking. Retrieved October 11, 2023, from https://www.buckleyschool.com/magazine/articles/calm-public-speaking-nerves-lets-talk-about-self-talk/#:

College, A., & News, R. L. (n.d.). Preparing great speeches: A 10-step approach | Sullivan | College & Research Libraries News. *Crln.acrl.org.* Retrieved October 12, 2023, from https://crln.acrl.org/index.php/crlnews/article/view/19102/22119#:

8 strategies to engage your audience & keep them interested. (n.d.). Www.knowledgehut.com. https://www.knowledgehut.com/blog/learning/8-strategies-to-engage-your-audience-keep-them-interested

Engaging and energizing audiences through purposeful play: An Interactive Exercises Model And Method. (n.d.). MentalHelp.net. Retrieved October 21, 2023, from https://www.mentalhelp.net/blogs/engaging-and-energizing-audiences-through-purposeful-play-an-interactive-exercises-model-and-method/#: %20Empathic%20Icebreaker

5 (NLP) Neurolinguistic programming techniques. (n.d.). Retrieved October 21, 2023, from https://www.tonyrobbins.com/leadership-impact/nlp-techniques/#:

Guarino, Joseph. "Top 20 Public Speaking Quotes." Institute of Public Speaking. Accessed November 16, 2023. https://www.instituteofpublicspeaking.com/top-20-public-speaking-quotes/

How thoughts drive fear. (n.d.). Explorable.com. Retrieved September 26, 2023, from https://explorable.com/e/how-thoughts-drive-fear#:

How to speak with confidence in public. (n.d.). Virtualspeech.com. Retrieved October 12, 2023, from https://virtualspeech.com/blog/speak-with-confidence-in-public#:

MindTools | Home. (n.d.). Www.mindtools.com. Retrieved October 18, 2023, from https://www.mindtools.com/agssrjn/the-five-canons-of-rhetoric#:

Nieuwhof, C. (2019, November 20). *The 4 different communication styles and how each can improve.* CareyNieuwhof.com. https://careynieuwhof.com/the-4-different-communication-styles-and-how-each-can-improve/#:

The psychology of fear. (n.d.). Verywell Mind. Retrieved September 26, 2023, from https://www.verywellmind.com/the-psychology-of-fear-2671696#:

Public speaking: Know your audience. (n.d.). Www.asme.org. Retrieved October 17, 2023, from https://www.asme.org/topics-resources/content/public-speaking-know-your-audience#:

Rice, A. (2021, September 13). *Challenging negative thoughts: Helpful tips.* Psych Central. https://psychcentral.com/lib/challenging-negative-self-talk#how-to-stop

Speech topics: Guide to choosing a successful topic. (n.d.). Virtualspeech.com. Retrieved October 18, 2023, from https://virtualspeech.com/blog/guide-choosing-successful-speech-topic#:

10.4: Organizing Your Speech | Introduction to public communication. (n.d.). Retrieved October 18, 2023, from http://kell.indstate.edu/public-comm-intro/chapter/10-4-organizing-your-speech/#:

31 fear of public speaking statistics (Prevalence). (n.d.). Www.crossrivertherapy.com. Retrieved September 26, 2023, from https://www.crossrivertherapy.com/public-speaking-statistics#:

Tips & guides - Engaging your audience. (n.d.). Hamilton College. Retrieved October 20, 2023, from https://www.hamilton.edu/academics/centers/oral communication/guides/how-to-engage-your-audience-and-keep-them-with-you#:

What is natural language processing (NLP) & how does it work? (n.d.). Levity.ai. Retrieved October 21, 2023, from https://levity.ai/blog/how-natural-language-processing-works#:

Made in the USA
Monee, IL
02 June 2024

59248383R10090